GREAT TED TALKS

INNOVATION

Portable Press
An imprint of Printers Row Publishing Group
10350 Barnes Canyon Road, Suite 100, San Diego, CA 92121
www.portablepress.com • mail@portablepress.com

Printers Row Publishing Group is a division of Readerlink Distribution Services, LLC.
Portable Press is a registered trademark of Readerlink Distribution Services, LLC.

Correspondence regarding the content of this book should be sent to Portable
Press, Editorial Department, at the above address. Author, illustration, and rights
inquiries should be sent to Quarto Publishing Plc, 6 Blundell St, London N7 9BH,
www.quartoknows.com.

Portable Press
Publisher: Peter Norton • Associate Publisher: Ana Parker
Editor: JoAnn Padgett
Senior Product Manager: Kathryn C. Dalby

Produced by Quarto Publishing Plc
Publisher: Mark Searle
Creative Director: James Evans
Art Director: Katherine Radcliffe
Commissioning Editor: Sorrel Wood
Managing Editor: Isheeta Mustafi and Jacqui Sayers
In-house Editor: Abbie Sharman
Editor: Anna Southgate
Designer: Matt Windsor

Library of Congress Control Number:2019951060
ISBN: 978-1-64517-216-1

Printed in China

24 23 22 21 20   1 2 3 4 5

GREAT
TED
TALKS

INNOVATION

An Unofficial Guide with
Words of Wisdom from
100 TED Speakers

NEIL C. HUGHES

**PORTABLE
PRESS**

San Diego, California

CONTENTS

> **INNOVATION HAPPENS WHEN PEOPLE ARE GIVEN THE FREEDOM TO ASK QUESTIONS AND THE RESOURCES AND POWER TO FIND THE ANSWERS.**
> **RICHARD BRANSON**

INTRODUCTION

What is innovation? And how do you become more innovative? A quick search online delivers hundreds of definitions that may leave you feeling confused. Spend too long soul-searching, and you could run the risk of falling into the analysis paralysis trap.

 The reality is that we are all trying to keep our heads above water in an era of unprecedented change. More than five years have passed since IBM's Bridget van Kralingen said, "The last best experience that anyone has anywhere, becomes the minimum expectation for the experience they want everywhere."

Welcome to the age of the experience economy. This is now a digital world in which businesses must adapt and evolve in order to meet the rising expectations of their customers. Measures that delivered success in the past could be responsible for your downfall in the future. But innovation can enable you to turn an idea, or even a friction point, into a solution that brings additional value to the world.

Looking for innovation blind spots and helping your team members find their creative sparks is a notoriously bumpy roller-coaster ride. Before trying to navigate uncharted territory alone, however, you can follow in the footsteps of other innovators and learn from their successes and failures.

TED Talks influence, teach, and inspire through the medium of storytelling. The stories we share unite people and ideas. They enable us to explore new approaches. In this book, you will learn from more than 100 TED speakers, who share their experiences with innovation.

Rule breakers who listen to their customers have an uncanny ability to see the world from multiple perspectives. By embracing a diversity of thought and failing fast, such people have already fueled innovation in their industry. But remember, innovation is a journey, not a destination. Embark on this journey through each stage of the innovation process and learn how some of the greatest innovative minds of our time achieved their successes. After reading this book, you will be ready to follow your own path in creating a story of your own.

HOW TO USE THIS BOOK

This book of tips is designed to be quick and easy to peruse. You can read it from front to back or back to front, or dip in and out whenever you need inspiration—it's completely up to you. And if you want to refer back to a tip later but can't remember where it is, that's no problem. At the back of the book are two indexes—one for topics, and one for the speakers quoted—so it's always easy to find what you're looking for.

Crucially, you don't need to have seen a single TED talk to enjoy this book. But maybe you'd like to deepen your learning and watch one of the talks now? Again, that's no problem, as at the time of publication, all of the talks are available to watch free online.

You will find the links to the talks included in this book as part of the speaker index. Or you can simply go to ted.com, click on the magnifying glass in the right-hand corner, and type in the title of the talk. For example, to find the first talk mentioned in the book (on page 10), you'd type "How to Find a Wonderful Idea."

Occasionally, though, a talk might not be there. During the production of this book, a few of them hadn't yet made it onto the TED website. Don't worry: they're all available to view on YouTube too. In other words, if a talk doesn't come up when you type it into ted.com, go to YouTube.com and search there instead. In this case, be sure to put the title in quote marks (" ") so that YouTube knows exactly what it's looking for (there are a few billion other videos on the site, so it pays to be specific).

Alternatively, you might prefer to type the title into Google (again, surrounded by quote marks). In that case, the talk should appear in Google's listings under the "Videos" heading.

Whether you choose simply to read the book or use it as a stepping-stone to the wider universe of watching TED talks, it's time to open your mind and be inspired. Prepare to get a whole new perspective on your profession and where it can take you!

THAT ELUSIVE INNOVATIVE IDEA

Root out the innovation blind spots in your business.

You are right. For the most part, it has all been done before. But innovation often involves taking what you already have and transforming existing or unoriginal ideas into something entirely new. Some of the best innovations are opportunities that arise from happy accidents. This chapter explores how, just by thinking differently and embracing serendipity, you can help innovation to flourish in your organization.

FINDING A WONDERFUL IDEA

Looking for surprises can unlock innovation in your organization.

Discussing analysis paralysis in his talk, entrepreneur Teagan Adams suggests it is the result of being flooded with information and choice. We often don't know when to start, but disaster can be averted by taking a step in the right direction.

Credited with revolutionizing the music video, rock band OK Go makes a good example to follow. The group accepts that you shouldn't plan everything, but should invite serendipity into the creative process. By combining planning with the art of experimentation, the band has been able to leverage wonder and surprise while avoiding getting bogged down in rigid processes. In the group's own talk, lead singer Damian Kulash talks of the frustrations of experimentation along with the conflicts caused by surprises and happy accidents.

"So, we're not just looking for good ideas, we're looking for good ideas that surprise us in some way. And this causes something of a problem, because the process that we all use to make stuff actually has a very strong bias against surprising ideas."

By expecting surprises and accepting that not everything needs to be planned, maybe you can bring your ideas to life, too.

> **THE REASON WE'VE HAD TROUBLE DESCRIBING HOW WE THINK OF THESE IDEAS IS THAT IT DOESN'T FEEL LIKE WE THINK OF THEM AT ALL. IT FEELS LIKE WE FIND THEM.**
> **DAMIAN KULASH**

🔍 FIND OUT MORE

OK Go's talk:
"How to Find a Wonderful Idea"
2017

Also try Teagan Adams's talk:
"Stop the Analysis Paralysis, Start Massive Momentum"
2018

HAPPY ACCIDENTS

Remove the fear of getting it wrong and embrace chance discoveries when innovating.

What do you want to be when you grow up? What are you going to do with your life? From a young age, we are told that if we fail to plan, we plan to fail. Yet, despite our best efforts to control our destiny, sometimes it feels as if the universe gives us a gentle nudge in the right direction.

There are many examples of chance encounters that lead to the discovery of a new job opportunity by accident. But why not consider intentional serendipity? When attempting to innovate, learn to expand your view and open yourself up to new ideas and ways of thinking.

Unlike rigid plans, chance events unlock new paths that can be tweaked along the way. CEO of start-up accelerator Matter Ventures, Corey Ford uses his talk to highlight how real innovation is a journey rather than a destination. "Taking little action, experimental steps, learning and adjusting, so that you end up in a place that you could never have predicted."

"We need people who don't know what they want to be when they grow up," Ford adds, "people who can sit with the fear and the ambiguity and who believe in intentional serendipity."

In his talk, entrepreneur Paul Hannam talks about how The Beatles and The Rolling Stones arose from serendipity. He tells us that we, too, should appreciate the accidental experiences that grace our lives.

> **INNOVATION AND ENTREPRENEURSHIP ARE ALL ABOUT HOW YOU INCREASE INTENTIONAL SERENDIPITY.**
> **COREY FORD**

🔍 FIND OUT MORE

Corey Ford's talk:
"Intentional Serendipity"
2013

Also try Paul Hannam's talk:
"Everyday Serendipity"
2016

CLIMB OUT OF YOUR BOX

Leave your ego behind and find the courage to step outside of your comfort zone.

 Step into any office in the world, and you will be surrounded by people operating inside the proverbial "box." Why? It's safe, and we take comfort in the familiarity of our daily routines. But we all know that one of the most dangerous phrases in the office is, "We've always done things this way."

Many people believe that they are not creative or innovative. They convince themselves that their IQ is not high enough or that they are "right-brain" thinkers. But such notions are nothing more than myths created by our own self-imposed limitations and boundaries. Frustrated by what is holding so many people back, founder of the Marconi Institute of Creativity, Giovanni Corazza, dared to explore what happens when you climb out of your comfort zone of misery to generate ideas.

In his talk, Corazza talks about ". . . a boundary within our minds, the boundary between what we know and what we haven't still or yet thought about creative thinking." The message from the talk is that you need to climb out of your box, let your mind wander (see page 20), and try to resist unfounded assumptions that prevent you from thinking creatively.

> **WE NEED TO BE FLUENT, LOOK FOR ALTERNATIVES, AND NOT FOR THE CORRECT ANSWER. BECAUSE WHEN YOU THINK CREATIVELY, THERE'S NO SINGLE CORRECT ANSWER.**
> **GIOVANNI CORAZZA**

Q FIND OUT MORE

Giovanni Corazza's talk: "How to Get Out of the Box and Generate Ideas" 2014

KNOW YOUR BLIND SPOTS

Find ways to identify and overcome deep-rooted cognitive biases.

Comedian Emo Philips once said, "I used to think the human brain was the most wonderful organ in my body. Then I realized who was telling me this." Noemie Delfassy founded Finer Flavors SA, a farm-fresh packaged-food company based in Geneva, Switzerland. She embarked on a mission of self-awareness to identify her own cognitive biases, or as she prefers to call them, blind spots.

In her talk, Delfassy speaks of the importance of being bold and enjoying the ride, but most importantly of all, ensuring that it's done with your eyes wide open. Where are your blind spots? Delfassy advises her audience that, "The powerful mind thinks it knows better. And it blinds us from seeing reality as it is. And we become stubborn in our ways."

Rather than hiding from imperfections, accept them and use them to your advantage. Remember that start-up founders don't fail, they learn. Changing your mind-set and identifying your blind spots will help enable you and your team to embed a culture of innovation. Consider this your wake-up call to face up to some hard truths and use it to remove any cognitive bias that is preventing innovation.

> **YOUR MIND CAN PLAY TRICKS ON YOU. BE AWARE OF THAT AND TRY TO BE PROACTIVE IN IDENTIFYING CERTAIN BIASES THAT YOU MAY HAVE.**
> **NOEMIE DELFASSY**

Q FIND OUT MORE

Noemie Delfassy's talk: "Where Are Your Blind Spots?" 2016

. . . .

RETHINK. REDEFINE. RE-CREATE.

Discover the art of innovation according to Guy Kawasaki.

Marketing specialist Guy Kawasaki told me that one of the biggest lessons he learned from working with Apple's Steve Jobs, is that customers are unable to give you the answers to help you innovate. Your audience will always ask you to make more of what you are already providing, preferably better, faster, and cheaper.

Kawasaki believes that one of the truths of innovation is being brave enough to jump to the next curve or even raise the bar and invent it. The art of innovation begins with the desire to create meaning. If you can change the world, you will also make money, he enthuses in his talk.

PepsiCo's John Sculley was of the same mind-set when he joined Steve Jobs at Apple, a company that set out to democratize computers and empower its customers (see page 16). Equally, eBay made it possible for anyone to enter the world of commerce and compete with any retailer. Google empowered people with information, while YouTube made it possible for the global community to create, upload, and share video content. This is just a handful of companies that have changed the world through innovation. It all began by rethinking, redefining, re-creating, and adding meaning to the world.

Although it can be tempting to follow the lead of your competitors, deep down, you know it's an incredibly shortsighted approach. Great innovation occurs when you don't limit yourself, and you think to the next curve. By daring to see things

> ## BOZOS ARE GOING TO TELL YOU IT CAN'T BE DONE, IT SHOULDN'T BE DONE, AND IT ISN'T NECESSARY, BUT DON'T LET THEM GRIND YOU DOWN.
>
> **GUY KAWASAKI**

differently and questioning the status quo, there will be some that cannot understand your vision. But Kawasaki offers some reassuring advice. Don't think about the process or product, but the benefits you provide your customers. In the tech world, it's engineers who create something that is unique and valuable. Marketing departments then convince the world that the finished product is indeed unique and valuable. That's how both money and history are made.

When embarking on your own innovation journey, remember: Don't listen to the naysayers. If someone tells you that you will fail and you listen to them, you will fail. Don't let them stop you.

Q FIND OUT MORE

Guy Kawasaki's talk:
"The Art of Innovation"
2014

BE CURIOUS AND TAKE RISKS

John Sculley reflects on a common trait shared by Bill Gates and Steve Jobs.

When I interviewed former PepsiCo president John Sculley in 2018, he told me how his early career with the company came to shape future innovations. Due to the overwhelming heat of the summer sun in Phoenix, he got up at 4:00 a.m. to learn the ropes. He drove Pepsi trucks and put up rooftop signs. He credited innovations, such as the creation of the first 2-liter (4¼-pint) plastic bottle and the Pepsi Challenge Campaign, to what he observed when he started out as a trainee.

In his talk, Sculley recalls the moment where Steve Jobs approached him and spoke the immortal line, "Do you want to sell sugar water for the rest of your life, or do you want to change the world with me?" Innovators are curious by nature, and

it was this curiosity that was a significant driver in Sculley following Steve Jobs to take a job with Apple.

In Silicon Valley, Sculley advised that anyone who made an embarrassing mistake or experienced failure should be asked the same question. "What did you learn?" Experience had taught Sculley that the mantra for innovation is simply to fail fast and fail forward. See Chapter 7 for a wider discussion on learning from failure.

Sculley's talk features an anecdote about being the fly on the wall during conversations between Steve Jobs and Bill Gates. From the outside looking in, many would have assumed that these two creative visionaries would be adversaries of sorts. But Sculley observed that they were not driven by money, power, and

> ## MY ADVICE IS ALWAYS TO BE CURIOUS, REACH OUT, AND TAKE RISKS.
> **JOHN SCULLEY**

competitiveness. As the CEO of Apple, Sculley was on the front line of a technological revolution, and he saw that innovation with a noble cause was the driving force. Both Gates and Jobs were motivated by creating computers that were a tool for the mind—a tool that could change the world by empowering one person at a time.

Sculley's time at Apple taught him lessons for every chapter of this book. Above all, perhaps, innovation should begin with a noble cause in its mission to change the world. If meaningful change is at the heart of what you set out to achieve, it becomes much easier to remove the fears associated with curiosity, risk-taking, and failure. To learn from innovators who have changed the world, see Chapter 10.

Q FIND OUT MORE

John Sculley's talk:
"Innovation With a Noble Cause"
2015

CHALLENGE YOURSELF

Dr. Amantha Imber presents an argument for focusing on challenges rather than ideas.

> **ONE OF THE PROBLEMS WITH INNOVATION IS THAT TOO MANY PEOPLE BELIEVE THAT IT'S A DICHOTOMY. YOU'RE EITHER BORN CREATIVE OR YOU'RE NOT CREATIVE. AND SO JUST BECOME AN ACCOUNTANT.**
>
> **DR. AMANTHA IMBER**

How do you access your inner innovator? Dr. Amantha Imber is an innovation psychologist, science nerd, and founder and CEO of Inventium. Using science-based methodology, the company has helped more than 200,000 people become better innovators and has promoted a culture in which innovation thrives. So where do most businesses go wrong?

According to Dr. Imber, seeking out challenges is the number one most impactful thing that you can do to drive innovation. So, rather than brainstorming for innovative ideas in a room full of people, you need to find challenges. When you feel challenged, you are 67 percent more likely to be innovative. So where should you begin?

In her talk, Dr. Imber advises "The first thing you need is a big challenge, something that excites you and maybe scares you too. You then need the skills. You need the right match between the challenge and the skill so that you've got the skills to rise to that challenge. And then

finally, you need the resources, time, and money to be able to solve that challenge."

In another talk, Dr. Imber seeks to educate her audience on how members can make efforts to access their own creative genius.

Having settled on a challenge to suit your personal skills—or the collective skills of your team members—you are more likely to find both the time and the resources to bring your vision to life.

🔍 FIND OUT MORE

Dr. Amantha Imber's talks: "Can You Design an Innovative Culture?" 2016

. . . .

"Accessing Your Creative Genius" 2011

THE WANDERING MIND

Don't forget to daydream and remember that boredom can lead to brilliance.

 In her talk, management consultant Christina Mackay highlights that the world's greatest theorists, innovators, and visionaries have one thing in common: they were daydreamers. But, when was the last time you allowed yourself to daydream? Given today's obsessions with binge viewing, gaming, and social media, many of us have forgotten how.

What actually happens to you when you get bored? Or, more importantly: What happens to you if you never get bored? And what could happen if you got rid of this human emotion entirely? These are a few questions that tech podcaster and author Manoush Zomorodi asked neuroscientists and cognitive psychologists.

Zomorodi quickly learned that when you get bored, "You ignite a network in the brain called the default mode. So, your body, it goes on autopilot while you're folding the laundry or you're walking to work, but actually, that is when your brain gets really busy."

There is a battle for your attention. The CEO of Netflix said, "Our biggest competitors are Facebook, YouTube, and sleep." But the real casualty of your obsession with staring at screens and endlessly scrolling is the art of daydreaming, which leads to creativity.

Don't be afraid to take a break, stare out the window, and know that by doing nothing you are actually being your most productive and creative self.

Q FIND OUT MORE

Manoush Zomorodi's talk: "How Boredom Can Lead to Your Most Brilliant Ideas" 2017

Also try Christina Mackay's talk: "The Magic Behind Daydreaming" 2016

" ONCE YOU START DAYDREAMING AND ALLOW YOUR MIND TO REALLY WANDER, YOU START THINKING A LITTLE BIT BEYOND THE CONSCIOUS, A LITTLE BIT INTO THE SUBCONSCIOUS, WHICH ALLOWS ALL SORTS OF DIFFERENT CONNECTIONS TO TAKE PLACE. **"**

DR. SANDI MANN, PSYCHOLOGIST

PROCRASTINATE!

Procrastination, fear, and doubt could just be the tools you need to help you succeed.

 Organizational psychologist Adam Grant was fascinated by creative thinkers who succeed in changing the world. He quickly learned that what sets innovators apart from everyone else is the frequency with which they fail. These are the ones who keep trying, who learn from their failures, and who continue to push forward.

In his talk, Grant states that "Even the three icons of classical music—Bach, Beethoven, Mozart—had to generate hundreds and hundreds of compositions to come up with a much smaller number of masterpieces." Just like everyone else, they're afraid of failing, but they're even more afraid of failing to try.

Ultimately, our biggest regrets are not our actions but our inactions—the things we wish we could redo. Procrastinators are often ridiculed and labeled as the leaders of tomorrow. But remember: even Leonardo da Vinci wrote in his journal that he felt like a failure after taking sixteen years to complete the *Mona Lisa*. Despite rewriting his speech at 3:00 a.m., Martin Luther King, Jr. decided to go off-script at the last minute and uttered four words that changed the course of history: "I have a dream." Grant argues, "You call it procrastinating. I call it thinking."

Just like you, the greatest innovators and creative thinkers feel fear and doubt. They procrastinate. They have bad ideas. But these qualities help them succeed and can help you do the same.

Q FIND OUT MORE

Adam Grant's talk: "The Surprising Habits of Original Thinkers" 2016

"

TO BE ORIGINAL, YOU DON'T HAVE TO BE FIRST. YOU JUST HAVE TO BE DIFFERENT AND BETTER. **"**

ADAM GRANT

EXPLORATION AND EXPLOITATION

To embark on a journey of innovation, you must be prepared to go on a journey into the unknown.

Is it possible to run a company and reinvent it at the same time? This is a question business strategist Knut Haanaes asked the audience of his talk. The reality is that most companies become less innovative as they become more competent. But in a digital age where companies must disrupt or be disrupted, something has to change.

Netflix famously built a thriving business by sending DVDs through the mail to millions of subscribers. It even offered itself for acquisition to Blockbuster for $50 million; Blockbuster declined the offer, and we all know how that story ended. In his talk, Haanaes advises, "I think they will always keep pushing for the next battle."

By merely embracing exploration and exploitation, it becomes much easier to run a successful business and innovate at the same time. Exploration is about coming up with what's new. It's about search and it's about discovery. It's about new products, it's about new innovations. It's about changing your frontiers.

By contrast, exploitation is taking the knowledge you have and making good, better. Exploitation is about making trains run on time. It's about making improved products faster and cheaper. Balancing exploration and exploitation will help prevent your business from falling into the success traps and running on autopilot.

FIND OUT MORE

Knut Haanaes's talk: "Two Reasons Companies Fail —and How to Avoid Them" 2016

> **"WHETHER YOU'RE AN EXPLORER BY NATURE OR WHETHER YOU TEND TO EXPLOIT WHAT YOU ALREADY KNOW, DON'T FORGET: THE BEAUTY IS IN THE BALANCE."**
>
> **KNUT HAANAES**

UNLOCKING THE CREATIVE SPARK

Discover how to develop a culture of innovation.

Contrary to popular belief, groundbreaking ideas are not confined to the minds of elite teams of creative thinkers. Every one of us is armed with an innovative mind-set and a creative spark. It's just that we often leave it to those who are more willing to take the lead. This chapter explores how innovation leadership can help unlock the creativity that drives innovative ideas. With this in place, you can build a culture of innovation in which the best ideas, rather than loudest voices, will win.

PUT PEOPLE FIRST

Inclusivity has a critical role to play in today's innovation strategy.

There is no escaping the impact of innovation in our lives or in the office. Emerging technologies are paving the way for new start-ups that could disrupt your current business model if you stand still. In an era of exponential change, many make the mistake of focusing on technology, but it's people that should be at the heart of any innovation strategy.

Organizational change expert Jim Hemerling thinks adapting your business in today's constantly evolving world can be invigorating instead of exhausting. In his talk, Hemerling discusses five imperatives centered around putting people first. He suggests that investment in innovation should not be built around developing new products or services.

It should be about inspiring employees through purpose and not being afraid to go all in to make a difference. Nurturing autonomy (see page 56) and instilling a culture of continuous learning will enable employees to develop the capabilities they need to succeed during the transformation and beyond. Everyone should feel that they have a voice and can make a difference, not just the big personalities.

> **" IN ORDER TO CAPTURE THE HEARTS AND MINDS OF PEOPLE, YOU ALSO NEED TO BE INCLUSIVE. "**
> **JIM HEMERLING**

Q FIND OUT MORE

Jim Hemerling's talk:
"Five Ways to Lead in an Era of Constant Change"
2016

EMBRACE DIVERSITY OF THOUGHT

Diversity and inclusion are crucial when building a culture of innovation.

If you are serious about serving a diverse customer base, you are going to need a team that celebrates diversity of thought. Online audiences visiting your website or following your tweets will be from a variety of cultures and backgrounds—and each person will have a unique mind-set.

The big questions are: Are diverse organizations more innovative? Can diversity be more than something to comply with? Can it be a real competitive advantage? Management consultant and diversity researcher Rocío Lorenzo, surveyed 171 companies, and the answer was a resounding yes to all of the above.

When Lorenzo looked at the data from her research, she discovered that "Companies that are more diverse are more innovative, and companies that are more innovative have more diverse leadership." She went on to state in her talk, "So it's fair to assume that it works both ways, diversity driving innovation and innovation driving diversity."

Lorenzo also explains that her "goal is to change the face of leadership, to make it more diverse—and not so that leaders can check a box and feel like they have complied with something or they have been politically correct. But because they understand. They understand that diversity is making their organization more innovative, better."

By treating diversity as a competitive advantage you will provide a genuine opportunity for everyone. For a wider discussion on diversity of thought, see Chapter 8.

> **THE DATA IN OUR SAMPLE SHOWED THAT MORE DIVERSE COMPANIES ARE SIMPLY MORE INNOVATIVE, PERIOD.**
> **ROCÍO LORENZO**

Q FIND OUT MORE

Rocío Lorenzo's talk:
"How Diversity Makes Teams More Innovative"
2017

GIVE VOICE TO THE MASSES

Leading innovation is not just about creating a vision and inspiring others to execute it.

> **"INNOVATION IS A JOURNEY. IT'S A TYPE OF COLLABORATIVE PROBLEM SOLVING, USUALLY AMONG PEOPLE WHO HAVE DIFFERENT EXPERTISE AND DIFFERENT POINTS OF VIEW. "**
>
> **LINDA HILL**

Linda Hill is a business professor whose ambition has been to help people learn to lead. Much to her surprise, she discovered that what many of us think of as great leadership does not work when it comes to leading innovation. Our world has dramatically changed and it's time to pave the way for a new form of leadership.

After studying leaders in twelve different industries across the globe, Hill arrived at a conclusion that surprised her.

"If we want to build organizations that can innovate time and again, we must unlearn our conventional notions of leadership."

In her talk, Hill explains how, "When many of us think about innovation, we think about Einstein having an 'Aha!' moment. But we all know that's a myth. Innovation is not about solo genius. It's about collective genius." In a nutshell, you need to listen to the voice of all employees and give them the tools to bring their innovative ideas to life.

What we know is, at the heart of innovation is a paradox. You have to unleash the talents and passions of many people, and you have to harness them into work that is useful. For these reasons alone, innovation strategy needs an entirely different form of leadership—one that embraces the "collaborative community" (see page 32) and enables the minority voices in your organization to speak up and be heard.

Q FIND OUT MORE

Linda Hill's talk:
"How to Manage for Collective Creativity"
2014
· ·

THE COLLABORATIVE COMMUNITY

A working environment that centers on collaboration and contribution is crucial for leaders.

We can find the answer to almost any question with the click of a button, swipe of our smartphone, or by simply using our voice. A student's idea of an encyclopedia is one that he or she can change and contribute to. We already share innovative ideas across a collaborative community. Why should our work life be any different?

When creating a corporate culture of collaborative innovation, Claire Madden has a clear message for future leaders of digital natives who cannot remember a time before the iPhone. "Traditional leadership styles have been based on linearity and conformity based on position and hierarchy. However, the leadership styles that the younger generations respond more to are those based on collaboration and contribution, where they can participate and have a voice."

Successful leaders in a digital age understand that we are designed to connect and contribute. For example, Airbnb took an innovative approach to accommodation. By leveraging the collaborative power of the community, anyone can become an accommodation provider and six million people already are.

What makes TED such a powerful brand? Sure, it's a combination of innovation, communication, and the spreading of ideas. But Madden also believes "it's released over to the collaborative community to take part in the model of TEDx events, and with local communities being able to take part. It's then maximized through the communication over the technology platforms."

Q FIND OUT MORE

Claire Madden's talk:
"Creating a Culture of
Collaborative Innovation"
2015

"

SOMETHING HAPPENS WHEN WE CONNECT FACE TO FACE. INTERACTION AND IDEAS AS SPARKS AND KNOWLEDGE ARE TRANSFERRED IN A WAY THAT ONLY HAPPENS IN THAT CONTEXT. WE ARE DESIGNED TO CONTRIBUTE. "

CLAIRE MADDEN

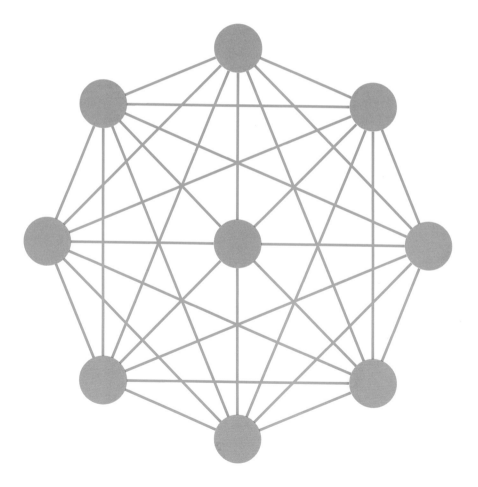

15/100
LEARN BY LISTENING

You don't need to have all the answers when collaboration is driving innovation.

Television and radio host Larry King once said, "I remind myself every morning: Nothing I say this day will teach me anything. So, if I'm going to learn, I must do it by listening." Businesses are learning that, by listening to both their customers and their employees, they can innovate to stay ahead of the curve.

A common misconception is that innovation is confined to a few creative types and professionals. The smartphone changed all that. Anyone can now create audio, video, photographic, and written content and share it with the world without the need to carry around expensive equipment.

When Charles Leadbeater began his career in journalism with the *Financial Times*, he recalls the excitement of seeing someone reading the newspaper on the London Underground. In these much simpler times, commuters would pick up a newspaper and read what was written for them. But now, those same readers want to be writers and publishers themselves.

Leadbeater's talk was back in 2005, yet it still provides excellent insights into how the best ideas are coming back from consumers who are often considerably further ahead than businesses. As a result, many are turning users into producers and consumers into designers of future products or services.

> **THERE IS A HUGE COMPETITIVE ARGUMENT ABOUT SUSTAINING THE CAPACITY FOR OPEN-SOURCE AND CONSUMER-DRIVEN INNOVATION BECAUSE IT'S ONE OF THE GREATEST COMPETITIVE LEVERS AGAINST MONOPOLY.**
> **CHARLES LEADBEATER**

🔍 FIND OUT MORE

Charles Leadbeater's talk: "The Era of Open Innovation" 2005

· ·

LOOK INWARDLY

By examining negativity arising from a change in the workplace, you can find ways to ease the transition.

An increasing number of organizations have a vision for a modern workplace that fosters collaboration, innovative thinking, and a productive workforce. Knowing what you want to build and how you want to change the world is the easy part. Achieving it is a little tricker.

Leadership coach Jude Reggett believes that "We need to create (or discover) the methods that deal with change and upset so that people around us become closer and supportive rather than defensive or aggressive. That process requires us to understand principles that affect our behavior, feelings, and thoughts."

In her talk, Reggett tackles some of the biggest questions facing organizations that set out on a journey of innovation. The usual starting points are: What does it take to deal with change? And, what does it take to be creative and innovative? The reality is that both take time and require additional resources.

Dr. Ramya Ranganathan agrees and in her talk discusses how we can change our thinking habits to cultivate a spirit of innovation within oneself.

> **IS IT ABOUT LOOKING INWARD? AND DOES CREATIVE ACTIVITY MEAN STOPPING THE BLAME GAME? LOOKING INSIDE YOURSELF, MAYBE YOU HAVE THE ANSWER?**
> **JUDE REGGETT**

🔍 FIND OUT MORE

Jude Reggett's talk:
"Fostering Creativity and Innovation in the Workplace"
2013

Also try Ramya Ranganathan's talk:
"Cultivating an Innovation Mind-Set for Life"
2017

LOOKING FOR A CREATIVE SPARK? TAKE A WALK!

Taking a walk can help your employees be more innovative.

 How can we be more innovative? This question is repeated in meeting rooms all over the world. Brainstorming sessions often result in awkward silences. The creative process that takes an idea to the final product is a painfully long process. But getting ideas out of everyone's heads is even more challenging.

Maybe you're doing it all wrong. What if you broke out of your restrictive creative space and went for a "walk and talk" with a couple employees instead? Research by behavioral and learning scientist Marily Oppezzo suggests that going for a walk might be all it takes to get your team's creative juices flowing.

In her talk, Oppezzo suggests that "First, you want to pick a problem or a topic to brainstorm. So, this is not the shower effect, when you're in the shower and all of a sudden, a new idea pops out of the shampoo bottle. This is something you're thinking about ahead of time. You're intentionally thinking about brainstorming a different perspective on the walk."

We are all surrounded by a myriad of digital distractions. By putting the tech down, you might find that walking and talking will help you get the most out of your next brainstorming session.

Q FIND OUT MORE

Marily Oppezzo's talk:
"Want to Be More Creative? Go for a Walk"
2017
. . . .

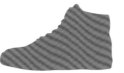

"

ONE KEY OF CREATIVITY IS TO NOT LOCK ON THAT FIRST IDEA. KEEP GOING. KEEP COMING UP WITH NEW ONES, UNTIL YOU PICK ONE OR TWO TO PURSUE. "

MARILY OPPEZZO

DON'T FAIL, LEARN

Some of your biggest frustrations and failures could help you to innovate.

 Encouraging a culture that enables all employees to help make your business more innovative is incredibly exciting in the beginning. Challenges and problems can quickly lead to frustration, however, and might even threaten to derail your efforts. But when did we fall out of love with things not going our way?

Children are widely regarded as being more innovative than adults. They are not fazed by the seemingly impossible or what doesn't work, and they carry on regardless. Creativity often arises from frustration. Some of the most successful start-ups emerge from a founder wanting to solve a problem he or she has encountered.

In his talk, economics writer Tim Harford tells the story of how musician Keith Jarrett found himself in front of a packed house at the Cologne Opera House, faced with an almost unplayable piano because all of the black keys were sticking. Jarrett was forced to avoid the upper registers, using only the middle tones of the keyboard. This unique way of playing created a different sound and resulted in a more energetic performance, which the crowd loved. *The Köln Concert* went on to be both the best-selling piano album and the best-selling solo jazz album in history.

Maybe it's time to embrace your randomness and frustration and to turn accident into opportunity (see page 11). Awaken your inner child—or, as Harford would say, "From time to time, we all need to sit down and try and play the unplayable piano."

Q FIND OUT MORE

Tim Harford's talk:
"How Frustration Can Make Us More Creative"
2016

"

WE NEED TO RUN STUPID EXPERIMENTS. WE NEED TO DEAL WITH THE AWKWARD STRANGERS. THESE THINGS HELP US. THEY HELP US SOLVE PROBLEMS, AND THEY HELP US BE MORE CREATIVE. "

TIM HARFORD

FIND THE RIGHT INGREDIENTS

How Joachim Horn reinfused technological engineering with joy and ease, so anyone can cook-up innovation.

What would happen if you tackled engineering in the same way as you approached cooking? Joachim Horn developed his own recipe using ingredients that can be easily mixed to make smart technology. He has made it easy for anyone to be an inventor using units that connect objects to each other and the internet.

In his talk, Horn reveals how he created a company named after his younger brother. He called it SAM labs. Horn compared his ingredients to Lego® for the iPad generation. "The more you use them, the easier the engineering gets, the more fun you have, and the more innovative your ideas become."

A few tech ingredients enabled Horn to bring a camera, the internet, and Twitter all into the same frame for his creation. However, it's what other people did with it that really blew him away. The internet of Things toolset enables every user to become an inventor and is a perfect example of how thinking differently can empower millions of people.

Horn highlighted that easy-to-use tech ingredients can not only bring ideas to life, but they can also unleash the would-be engineer in anyone.

Q FIND OUT MORE

Joachim Horn's talk:
"An Easy Way to Cook Up Innovation"
2015

Also try Pietro Carnevale's talk:
"A Tasty Corporate Innovation Pizza"
2018

"

**FOR KIDS PLAYING
AROUND THEIR HOUSE
TO HACK THINGS
TOGETHER, OR ADULTS
CREATING ENTIRELY
NEW PRODUCTS, THEY
NEED THE RIGHT
INGREDIENTS. "**

JOACHIM HORN

THAT EUREKA MOMENT

Find out where innovative ideas come from and learn how you can replicate them.

 We have all experienced a flash of insight or an epiphany. These light bulb moments suggest that an idea is a single thing; often it's something that happens in a beautiful illuminating moment. But author Steven Johnson believes it's often much more complicated than that.

In his talk, Johnson advises, "We take ideas from other people, from people we've learned from, from people we run into in the coffee shop, and we stitch them together into new forms and we create something new. That's where innovation happens."

Google employees are encouraged to work on whatever they want for 20 percent of their time in the office. The policy inspires innovative projects and brings people together. Often these hunch-cultivating mechanisms create something completely different when several ideas are put into one big pot. By incentivizing employees to come up with more ideas, the culture is naturally more innovative.

Johnson believes in the unplanned emergent, unpredictable power of open innovative systems: "When you build them right, they lead to new directions that the creators never even dreamed of."

Seventh-grader Sarah Darby offers an alternative school of thought and suggests that it has all been done before. For her, the real groundbreaking innovation resides in how you piece together the fragments of those old ideas.

🔍 FIND OUT MORE

Steven Johnson's talk:
"Where Good Ideas Come From"
2010

Also try Sarah Darby's talk:
"All Our Ideas Come From Fragments"
2018

" "

**THAT IS HOW INNOVATION
HAPPENS. CHANCE FAVORS
THE CONNECTED MIND. " "**
STEVEN JOHNSON

FIGHTING THE FEAR OF CHANGE

Rewards await on the other side of fear.

Despite living in a digital age of exponential change, fear of innovation continues to hold back individuals and entire companies. Innovation is not about providing a platform for self-appointed creatives to lead the way; it's about ensuring that everyone within your organization feels comfortable about putting his or her innovative ideas forward. This chapter encourages us to look into our deepest darkest fears and understand what they can teach us about how to succeed with innovation.

DISRUPT OR BE DISRUPTED

Leaders should be afraid of inaction rather than action.

Uber disrupted the global taxi industry without owning a single car. The world's largest accommodation provider, Airbnb, is currently offering six million rooms but it doesn't own any property. Equally, retailer Alibaba doesn't carry any stock. How can businesses replicate the same spirit of hyper-innovation?

Business transformation expert Stefan Gross-Selbeck asks the question, "How can a start-up consisting of just a few people and barely any resources outcompete a big global company when it comes to digital innovation?" One of the biggest things holding businesses back is accepting that failure is a part of reality.

In start-up life, the motto is "fail fast, succeed faster." Failure is embraced as a learning opportunity when racing ahead to secure a competitive advantage. Larger corporations are much more cautious and nervous about investing time and resources into new ways of working.

In his talk, Gross-Selbeck offers a warning to businesses that are fearful of change: "If you are a manager in a big company, I think you have a choice. You can either try to look and learn from start-ups and improve your ability to discover new business models. Or just sit back and relax and watch how software eats the world until someone makes your lunch." It seems to me that the only thing to be afraid of is doing nothing at all.

> **ASK YOURSELF, WHAT DOES IT TAKE TO DISRUPT YOUR BUSINESS MODEL, TAKE YOUR VALUE CHAIN, AND CUT IT INTO PIECES AND PUT IT TOGETHER IN A DIFFERENT WAY.**
> **STEFAN GROSS-SELBECK**

Q FIND OUT MORE

Stefan Gross-Selbeck's talk: "Business Model Innovation: Beating Yourself at Your Own Game" 2014

FOSTER CREATIVITY

Reacquainting yourself with your inner child could unlock creative innovation.

 Picasso once said every child is an artist. The problem is staying an artist when you grow up.

Design leader Catherine Courage challenges leaders to drive innovation in the workplace by igniting their innate creativity from childhood.

As adults, we become laser-focused on execution, process, and efficiency. In doing so, we neglect innovation. In her talk, Courage states that, "We create cultures where we are afraid to fail. And as a result, we do the same thing again and again and again, because it's what we know, and it feels safe. But we aren't able to innovate by repeating the same thing, we get trapped in this cycle of micro improvements of incrementalism and missing out on that great opportunity for creative innovation."

As children, we questioned the world and were curious about everything. For example, the average preschooler asks one hundred questions a day. You can draw a lot of inspiration about creativity from your childhood. It starts by opening your mind, looking for new possibilities, and challenging the status quo.

Just like parents foster creativity in their children, so you must do the same in the workplace.

> " REMEMBER, CREATIVITY IS A BIRTHRIGHT. IT'S AVAILABLE TO ALL BUT USED BY FEW. "
> **CATHERINE COURAGE**

Q FIND OUT MORE

Catherine Courage's talk:
"Igniting Creativity to Transform Corporate Culture"
2012

23/100
DEFINE THE PROBLEM

Help your employees to understand the design thinking process.

 Few things can help transform a company more than a culture of innovation. Unsurprisingly, most leaders recognize the need to be more innovative. It's easy to become starry-eyed by the likes of tech giants Apple and Google, but every business has its own unique organizational culture.

But building a culture of innovation is notoriously difficult. Staff members often impose limitations on themselves. Some say that they are not creative or don't know how to be innovative. Get the balance wrong, and fear leads to anger. Anger leads to hate. Hate leads to suffering. So where should you start?

Cofounder of Tools at Schools, Don Buckley has transformed learning spaces, so that they work for teachers and students and not just the architects who design them. He has also transformed textbooks so that they work for students and teachers and not just the publishers. But he was only able to do this by getting everyone to embrace the design thinking process and, in doing so, to define the problem as a priority.

For Buckley, collaboration was key (see also page 32). In his talk, he shares how his organization pinned up more than one hundred problems in the school gym. Everyone could identify similar problems and became invested in the process of design thinking. These early steps were the building blocks of creating a culture of innovation that everybody understood.

Q FIND OUT MORE

Don Buckley's talk:
"Building a Culture of Innovation"
2013
. . . .
Also try Guido Stompff's talk:
"Speed Up Innovation with Design Thinking"
2016

> **IF YOU DON'T DEFINE THE PROBLEM, YOU END UP WITH A SOLUTION THAT ACTUALLY CREATES CHAOS AND DOESN'T REALLY FIX ANYTHING.**
> **DON BUCKLEY**

INNOVATE OR GO BUST

Has your business learned from the lessons of our digital past?

 Do you remember when Xerox, Kodak, Nokia, and Blockbuster appeared to be untouchable? Seemingly out of nowhere, they were blindsided by start-ups that disrupted their industry. The problem is that large a corporation can quickly become a prisoner of its own corporate structure, process, and culture. "If it isn't broke, don't fix it" is the mantra, and the entire corporate machine will continue doing exactly as it has done for years.

However, business model life cycles are much shorter than they used to be and preparing for an uncertain future has become a priority. In his talk, design thinker Joshua Lavra hammered home this point by highlighting that 88 percent of the Fortune 500 companies that existed fifty years ago no longer exist.

This does not mean that you cannot innovate within large organizations, however. By harnessing the entrepreneurial spirit inside of a company, it becomes much easier to maintain stable innovation. More and more businesses are adopting the lean start-up model. It focuses on building, measuring, and learning, and then going through this process again and again. Ultimately, it's about jumping into a problem, getting your ideas down, and sharing them with other people. The feedback you receive is the best way to drive your own reality.

🔍 FIND OUT MORE

Joshua Lavra's talk:
"Can You Innovate Within Large Organizations?"
2016

Also try Liam Tjoa's talk:
"Lessons Learned from the Snapchat-Age(d)"
2017

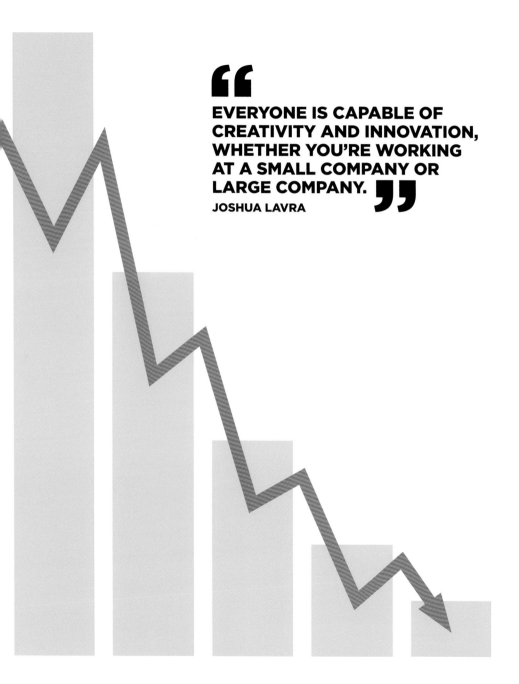

"EVERYONE IS CAPABLE OF CREATIVITY AND INNOVATION, WHETHER YOU'RE WORKING AT A SMALL COMPANY OR LARGE COMPANY. "

JOSHUA LAVRA

THINK POSITIVE

Why positive change should be at the heart of your innovation strategy.

 Fear of change can cripple an entire organization. Harvard Business School professor Rosabeth Moss Kanter has revealed six factors that are key to delivering positive change. It is not enough just to show up, she says. By speaking up and looking at the bigger vision, it becomes much easier to get everybody on board. It's also important to understand that you cannot do it all yourself. The most successful businesses surround themselves with successful partners, support, and lift others.

Most importantly of all, you should never give up. Kanter also offered a timely reminder to the audience that Nelson Mandela was in prison for twenty-seven years. He didn't give up and finally emerged from prison to become South Africa's first democratically elected president. What is your excuse for giving up so easily?

Innovation can add significant positive changes that will impact your entire organization. It's much more than introducing a new range of products or services. It could also be implementing new processes that reduce overheads or optimize efficiencies. Whatever the most pressing problems facing your business today, Kanter's six keys to leading positive change are a great place to start.

Q FIND OUT MORE

Rosabeth Moss Kanter's talk: "Six Keys to Leading Positive Change" 2013

“
FIND YOUR INNER MANDELA, FIND THE STRENGTH TO PERSIST, EVEN AGAINST THE NAYSAYERS, THE CRITICS, AND THE OBSTACLES, BECAUSE THAT'S WHAT MAKES THE DIFFERENCE BETWEEN SUCCESS AND FAILURE. „
ROSABETH MOSS KANTER

UNLEASH YOUR SUPERPOWERS

Becoming an inspiration to your employees will help eradicate fear.

 The illusion of always being busy often makes it feel as if there are just not enough hours in the day to complete your tasks. The concept of stopping to explore new ideas is a luxury that many inherently feel they cannot afford. But, creating a culture in which creativity flourishes and inspires innovative ideas should be at the top of the agenda for companies of all sizes.

In her talk, Ashley Haynes-Gaspar focuses her superpowers on creative strategy, innovation, and driving change. "I'm here today to talk to you about a superpower that is lurking within each of you. And it's a superpower of creativity and imagination. And by being able to harness those superpowers, you're in a position to lead transformative innovation within your businesses, and your organization."

When you're leading innovation within companies, it's critical that you pivot your thinking away from the idea of investing a lot of time and energy in figuring out if it's worth the risk, and toward simply taking that leap of faith and trying anyway because you have a belief in a better way. Innovation is not all about you; it's about everyone in your organization, so why not use your superpowers to inspire them?

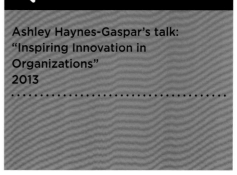

Q FIND OUT MORE

Ashley Haynes-Gaspar's talk: "Inspiring Innovation in Organizations" 2013

" WHEN YOU'RE LEADING INNOVATION WITHIN COMPANIES, IT'S ABSOLUTELY CRITICAL THAT YOU PIVOT YOUR THINKING. "

ASHLEY HAYNES-GASPAR

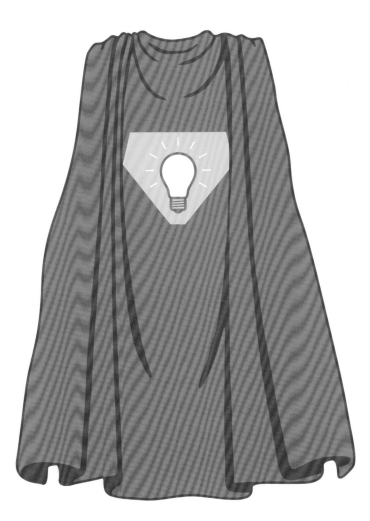

27/100
NURTURE AUTONOMY

Reboot your way of working to encourage autonomous decision-making at all levels.

 As we nervously move forward navigating unchartered digital waters, we all have to adapt and be prepared for change, or risk getting left behind. Transformation expert Martin Danoesastro shares the lessons he learned from companies on both sides of the innovation wave on how to structure an organization so that people at all levels feel empowered to make decisions quickly and respond to change.

In his talk, Danoesastro opens by asking the audience, "Have you ever watched a flock of birds work together? Thousands of animals, flying in perfect synchrony: isn't it fascinating? What I find remarkable is that these birds would not be able to do that if they all would have to follow one leader."

Scientists believe these birds rely on a few simple rules that allow every bird to make autonomous decisions while flying in perfect synchrony. Their alignment enables their autonomy, and their independence makes them fast and flexible. What if we humans could try something similar?

And if it really did empower people to make decisions more quickly, what would you be willing to give up?

Ira Wolfe is someone that describes himself as a "Millennial trapped in a Baby Boomer body." In his talk, he also encourages the audience to embrace the future that will be and move away from the past that was. He also offers a template of how to embrace change and make it work positively for you and your business.

Q FIND OUT MORE

Martin Danoesastro's talk: "What Are You Willing to Give Up to Change the Way We Work?" 2019

Also try Ira Wolfe's talk: "Make Change Work for You" 2016

> **IF WE WANT TEAMS TO BE FAST, FLEXIBLE, CREATIVE, LIKE A MINI-START-UP, THEY HAVE TO BE EMPOWERED AND AUTONOMOUS. BUT THIS MEANS WE CANNOT HAVE LEADERS COMMANDING THEIR PEOPLE WHAT TO DO.** "
>
> **MARTIN DANOESASTRO**

THE POWER OF INTROVERTS

Introverts bring extraordinary talents and abilities to the workplace and should be encouraged and celebrated.

Being an introvert used to be considered a negative trait. Thankfully we are starting to see the value that introverts bring to the workplace. In her talk, eleventh-grade student Asritha Swaminadhan reveals how research shows introverts are creative and curious critical thinkers making them a key part of any innovation journey.

Writer Susan Cain agrees. In her passionate talk, she argues that introverts bring extraordinary talents and abilities to the world and should be encouraged and celebrated in business.

Some say that the loudest person in the room is the weakest, while others believe that the quietest people have the loudest minds. Whatever side of the fence you find yourself, looking inwardly (see page 35) should be considered a virtue, not a problem.

Cain tells her audience that "Offices should be encouraging casual, chatty cafe-style types of interactions—you know, the kind where people come together and serendipitously have an exchange of ideas. It's great for introverts, and it's great for extroverts." However, she does warn that we need much more privacy, freedom,

and autonomy at work. Working together in a team is crucial, but both extroverts and introverts need to work on their own. Why? Because that is where deep thought comes from.

> **STOP THE MADNESS FOR CONSTANT GROUP WORK. JUST STOP IT.**
> **SUSAN CAIN**

Q FIND OUT MORE

Susan Cain's talk:
"The Power of Introverts"
2012

Also try Asritha Swaminadhan's talk: "Standing Out As an Introvert in a World of Extroverts"
2017

A FEAR OF ROBOTS

Develop a new leadership style that enables your employees to innovate.

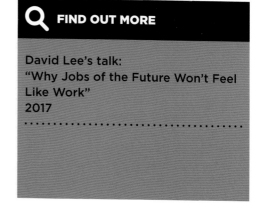

The role of technology and innovation in the workplace will not be embraced by everyone straight away. Automation and the fear of robots coming to take their jobs has understandably made people nervous about the next big company initiative.

Innovation expert David Lee says that we should start designing positions that unlock our hidden talents and passions. "I believe that the jobs of the future will come from the minds of people who today we call analysts and specialists, but only if we give them the freedom and protection that they need to grow into becoming explorers and inventors."

Lee's talk offers a wake-up call to managers who want their innovation strategies to be successful. "If we really want to robotproof our jobs, we, as leaders, need to get out of the mind-set of telling people what to do and instead start asking them what problems they're inspired to solve and what talents they want to bring to work."

Emerging technologies such as artificial intelligence (AI) and machine learning won't replace humans, they will set them free from repetitive, mundane, and robotic tasks. Your employees have a chance to showcase irreplaceable human skills such as creativity, innovation, and imagination. If you haven't told them this, it's about time you did.

> ❝ **WHEN YOU INVITE PEOPLE TO BE MORE, THEY CAN AMAZE US WITH HOW MUCH MORE THEY CAN BE.** ❞
> **DAVID LEE**

Q FIND OUT MORE

David Lee's talk:
"Why Jobs of the Future Won't Feel Like Work"
2017

THE INNOVATION DREAM TEAM

Discover the power of turning a group of strangers into a team.

To embed a culture of innovation across an entire organization, you will need to unite employees across multiple departments. It's the only way you will obtain buy-in and successfully retrieve ideas from individuals regardless of hierarchy or rank.

Business school professor Amy Edmondson studies "teaming," where a group of strangers is brought together and transformed into a quick-thinking team. In her talk, Edmondson talks about the elements required to complete goals. "You have to get different expertise at different times, you don't have fixed roles, you don't have fixed deliverables, you're going to be doing a lot of things that have never been done before, and you can't do it in a stable team."

Have you thought about how you can unite your organization and overcome corporate politics? Edmondson asks, "How quickly can you find the unique talents, skills, and hopes of your neighbor, and how quickly, in turn, can you convey what you bring? Because for us to team up to build the future, we know we can create what none of us can do alone, that's the mind-set we need."

In his talk, Matt Eng also offers a timely reminder that building successful teams is much more complicated than documenting people's skill sets. It is also essential to understand what motivates each person and his or her instincts. This is the best way to ensure everyone helps each other.

FIND OUT MORE

Amy Edmondson's talk:
"How to Turn a Group of Strangers Into a Team"
2017

Also try Matt Eng's talk:
"Teams Start with Human Connections"
2018

"

**IT'S AWFULLY HARD
TO TEAM IF YOU
INADVERTENTLY
SEE OTHERS AS
COMPETITORS.** "

AMY EDMONDSON

CUSTOMERS ARE THE ARCHITECTS OF INNOVATION

You need to find ways to navigate in this customer-centric age.

We live in an age of one-click checkouts, where we can access a favorite book, album, or movie with the swipe of a smartphone. It's not the big tech companies pushing these changes, however, but the users and their continuously rising expectations. By removing traditional pain points, the landscape now looks very different. Facebook doesn't create content, Alibaba has no inventory, and Airbnb has more rooms than any hotel chain but doesn't own any real estate. This chapter explores how, if you are serious about innovation, you should learn from your customers.

INNOVATION IN EVERYDAY LIFE

Your customers and employees will help you innovate.

By now, you should know that customer engagement helps drive innovation. But overthinking causes analysis paralysis and prevents you from moving quickly to make the most of emerging opportunities. What if I were to tell you two years ago, that millions of people would roam the streets overnight, looking for imaginary creatures?

Anyone that remembers the Pokémon Go craze a few years ago will recall that some businesses were able to gauge the customer reactions to the phenomenon and ride the wave to increase their revenues. By the time others finally decided to make a move, it turned into Pokémon Gone! Innovation is increasingly becoming everyone's responsibility within a company, and this is a message that needs to be amplified.

Entrepreneur Alex Goryachev has a simple mantra in life. "If you can imagine it, you can create it." In his talk, he reveals that the lonely innovator is a myth. "It takes teams of people to make things happen. And innovation is about inclusion and diversity. It's all about the rare art of listening to other people's ideas and coming together to make those ideas a reality."

Goryachev is clearly passionate about the ability to coinnovate with his customers. But, ultimately, "It's all about turning ideas into solutions that disrupt markets for social and economic good." But to do that you need to involve everyone and make a few mistakes along the way.

> **IF YOU'RE NOT PREPARED TO BE WRONG, YOU'LL NEVER COME UP WITH ANYTHING ORIGINAL.**
> **SIR KEN ROBINSON, EDUCATION REFORMER**

Q FIND OUT MORE

Alex Goryachev's talk: "Everyone Is an Entrepreneur—The Art of Innovation in Everyday Life" 2018

OUR THROWAWAY SOCIETY

What can you learn from a scrapyard in Ghana?

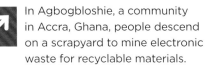 In Agbogbloshie, a community in Accra, Ghana, people descend on a scrapyard to mine electronic waste for recyclable materials. Upon closer inspection, there is an entire ecosystem emerging in which everyone is searching for something.

In his talk, cofounder of architecture and integrated design studio Low Design Office, DK Osseo-Asare advises that "Makers are searching for materials, parts, components, tools, blueprints to make what it is they want to make." Could we finally be moving away from the throwaway society that has caused so much damage on our planet?

DK Osseo-Asare believes that we need to begin by adjusting our language and mind-set. "A dump is a place where you throw things away and leave them forever; a scrapyard is where you take things apart. Waste is something that no longer has any value, whereas scrap is something that you recover specifically to use it to remake something new."

Environmentalist and innovator Binish Desai advises in his talk that the concept of "waste" does not exist in nature, but is generated by human consumption. As consumers, we need to stop looking at waste as being useless and learn how we can turn it into eco treasure.

> **"**
> **INNOVATION IS TAKING TWO THINGS THAT ALREADY EXIST AND PUTTING THEM TOGETHER IN A NEW WAY.**
> **TOM FRESTON, COFOUNDER OF MTV**

Q FIND OUT MORE

DK Osseo-Asare's talk:
"What a Scrapyard in Ghana Can Teach Us About Innovation"
2018

Also try Binish Desai's talk:
"Waste into Eco Treasure by the Recycle Man of India"
2018

33/100
TAKE A SHORTCUT

Learn to identify the desired path of your customers.

 When you take a stroll around your local park, you will probably notice paths around the edges that enable people to complete a circuit. Look a little closer, and you may also see a worn-out track right through the center of the park. Some people choose to take a shortcut rather than walk around the edge.

In his talk, venture capitalist Tom Hulme explains that such a shortcut is actually called a desire path. It's often the path of least resistance. He believes that these paths represent the point at which design and user experience diverge. Very often, city planners learn from these desire paths and pave over them. The relationship between your customers and how they use your products is very similar.

Hulme explains further, "I think empathy for what your customers want is probably the biggest leading indicator of business success. Design for real needs and design them in low friction, because if you don't offer them in low friction, someone else will, often the customer." In another talk

architect and designer William McDonough asks how our buildings and products might look if designers took into account "all children, all species, for all time."

Now that you know how to spot a desire path, you will start noticing them everywhere. They are going to spring up faster than ever. Your job is to pick the appropriate ones and pave over them.

FIND OUT MORE

Tom Hulme's talk: "What Can We Learn From Shortcuts?" 2016

Also try William McDonough's talk: "Cradle to Cradle Design" 2007

> **IF ANYBODY HERE HAS TROUBLE WITH THE CONCEPT OF DESIGN HUMILITY, REFLECT ON THIS: IT TOOK US FIVE THOUSAND YEARS TO PUT WHEELS ON OUR LUGGAGE.**
> **WILLIAM MCDONOUGH**

INNOVATION AND STRANGERS

Strangers can help you innovate.

> **THINK OF YOURSELF AS AN ATOM, BUMPING UP AGAINST OTHER ATOMS, TRANSFERRING ENERGY WITH THEM, BONDING WITH THEM A LITTLE, AND MAYBE CREATING SOMETHING NEW ON YOUR TRAVELS THROUGH THE SOCIAL UNIVERSE.**
>
> **TANYA MENON**

 Without even realizing it, most of us spend our time in narrow social circles with people similar to ourselves. In her talk, organizational psychologist Tanya Menon challenges everyone to look at their friends sitting next to them.

Menon then asks, "Are they of the same nationality as you? Are they of the same gender as you? Are they of the same race? Look at them closely. Don't they kind of look like you as well?" This is something that we all do subconsciously, and there is nothing wrong in feeling comfortable surrounding ourselves with like-minded souls.

The problem only occurs when our habits confine us and prevent us from expanding our social universes. At a time when you are exploring new ideas and opportunities, it's the person that you haven't met yet that could hold the key to successful innovation. Someone with a different worldview, ideas, and perspectives is often the most valuable person to spend time with.

One of the drawbacks of social media is that we surround ourselves with everything we like and remove everything we don't. Your innovation teams mustn't become echo chambers (see also page 60). Rethinking your relationships and developing habits that allow you to build positive connections with other people is where the real magic happens.

🔍 FIND OUT MORE

Tanya Menon's talk:
"The Secret to Great Opportunities? The Person You Haven't Met Yet"
2018

Also try Colin Easton's talk:
"The Impact of Strangers"
2014

THE REALM OF INVISIBLE INNOVATION

You can transform the customer experience by innovating the unseen processes.

Can India become a global hub for innovation? In his talk, Professor of Marketing Nirmalya Kumar argues that it already is. The rise of "invisible innovation" is enabling companies not just to outsource manufacturing jobs, but top management positions too.

For business customers, the traditional and much-maligned call center has been transformed by technology. Analytical tools armed with predictive modeling can predict what a given phone call is about before it's even answered.

Kumar passionately advises that process innovation is different than, but just as important as, product innovation. "It's about how do you create a new product, or develop a new product, or manufacture a new product, but not a new product itself." It's the innovations that we do not see that often deliver the most significant value."

In another talk, marketing and customer experience executive John Boccuzzi Jr. advises how he was seduced by exceptional customer service. Again, invisible innovation can make someone feel special during the buying journey. "This is such an important step and part of the customer journey, and if you get this right, it sets you up for future sales and a long-term customer relationship."

Innovation is much more than a shiny new gadget or something that you can see in the physical sense. Your most valuable innovations could be the processes that are invisible to your customers.

Q FIND OUT MORE

Nirmalya Kumar's talk:
"India's Invisible Innovation"
2012

Also try John Boccuzzi Jr.'s talk:
"I Was Seduced by Exceptional Customer Service"
2018

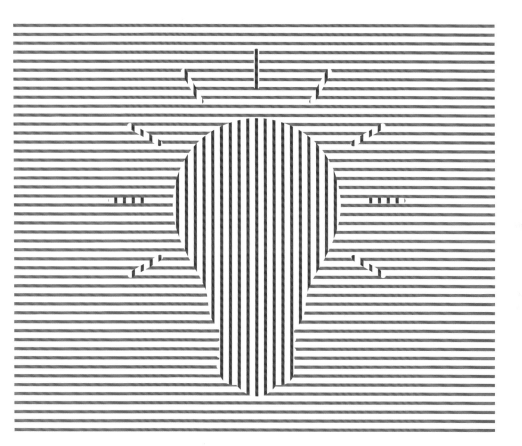

"

I THINK FRUGALITY DRIVES INNOVATION, JUST LIKE OTHER CONSTRAINTS DO. ONE OF THE ONLY WAYS TO GET OUT OF A TIGHT BOX IS TO INVENT YOUR WAY OUT.

"

JEFF BEZOS, FOUNDER OF AMAZON

THE CHANGING FACE OF RETAIL

Entire nations are going straight to mobile and innovating their way to success.

The world's most valuable retailer, Alibaba, does not carry stock. Five hundred million Chinese consumers regularly make purchases via mobile platforms, even in brick-and-mortar stores. It's clear that the future of retail isn't what it used to be.

Ultraconvenience and spontaneity are just a small part of the transformational change in retail. In China, a consumer would spend one hour on his or her smartphone shopping. That's three times higher than the time spent in the United States.

In her talk, retail expert Angela Wang explains how shopping behaviors and also technology platforms have evolved differently in China than elsewhere in the world. For example, e-commerce in China is soaring. It's been growing twice as fast as that of the United States. But the scale of e-commerce is not the issue here; it is the speed of adoption and the aggregation of the ecosystems.

It took China less than five years to become a country of mobile commerce. The rollout of high-speed mobile connectivity in emerging markets in developing countries such as India and in parts of Africa are also paving the way for an unprecedented era of opportunity.

Innovators have the tools to leapfrog the more traditional developmental stages in business to reap the rewards and accelerate their economic growth. As Fairphone founder Bibi Bleekemolen says in her talk, the cell phone has become a vehicle for change.

🔍 FIND OUT MORE

Angela Wang's talk:
"How China Is Changing the Future of Shopping"
2017
. . . .
Also try Bibi Bleekemolen's talk:
"How a Mobile Phone Became a Vehicle for Change"
2016

"

IF YOU HAVE A DIFFERENT MIND-SET, YOU WILL HAVE A DIFFERENT OUTCOME: IF YOU MAKE DIFFERENT CHOICES FROM YOUR PEERS, YOUR LIFE WILL THEN BE DIFFERENT FROM YOUR PEERS.

JACK MA, COFOUNDER
OF THE ALIBABA GROUP

"

ASK FOR HELP

Nobody innovates alone, so you better get used to asking your customers for help.

↗ It's ironic that in a digital age of seamless collaboration, most of us are scared to ask someone for help when we need it. For example, if you get lost while driving somewhere, rolling down your window and asking for help is usually at the bottom of the list. The bad news is that you cannot often innovate alone.

> **"**
> **SO, WHEN YOU NEED HELP, ASK FOR IT OUT LOUD. AND WHEN YOU DO, DO IT IN A WAY THAT INCREASES YOUR CHANCES THAT YOU'LL GET A 'YES' AND MAKES THE OTHER PERSON FEEL AWESOME FOR HAVING HELPED YOU, BECAUSE YOU BOTH DESERVE IT. 🙰**
>
> **HEIDI GRANT**

Heidi Grant researches, writes, and speaks about the science of motivation, influence, and decision-making. In her talk, she declares that "if we're going to ask for help—and we have to, we all do, practically every day—the only way we're going to get comfortable with it is to get good at it."

When you ask for help, Grant advises that you need to be very specific about the help you want and why. "Vague, sort of indirect requests for help actually aren't very helpful to the helper, right?"

In a bid to feel less awkward, don't take the impersonal route of text or email. It's not cool, and in-person requests for help are thirty times more likely to get a yes.

🔍 **FIND OUT MORE**

Heidi Grant's talk:
"How to Ask for Help—and Get a 'Yes.'"
2019

GIVE BACK TO SOCIETY

Today's focus is on creating an innovative strategy that makes a difference.

In her talk, Wendy Woods discusses corporate philanthropy and corporate social responsibility. "Total societal impact (TSI) is the sum of all of the ways business can affect society by doing the real work: thinking about their supply chains, working on their product design and manufacturing processes and their distribution."

Sure, business leaders might argue that their role is to ensure they meet the needs of their customers and to do so profitably. But Woods explains that "One of the best ways for businesses to help ensure their growth, their longevity, is to meet some of the hardest challenges in our society and to do so profitably."

Innovative businesses can create additional business benefits, exceed the expectations of their customers, and solve important problems in our world today. A creative and innovative corporate strategy should not be aimed solely at the customer. Richard Branson echoed these thoughts in his talk, where he reveals that his motivations also center around helping the global community (see page 185). There is an opportunity to make a difference, so why don't you take it?

> **IF YOU AREN'T MAKING A DIFFERENCE IN OTHER PEOPLE'S LIVES, YOU SHOULDN'T BE IN BUSINESS — IT'S THAT SIMPLE.**
> **RICHARD BRANSON**

Q FIND OUT MORE

Wendy Woods's talk:
"The Business Benefits of Doing Good"
2017

WORK WITH YOUR CUSTOMERS NOT AGAINST THEM

Finding your way in this customer-centric age will help you deliver true value.

 Way back in 2009, in the wake of the U.S. financial crisis of 2007–08, CEO and columnist John Gerzema delivered a talk about what he called the great unwind. With thirteen trillion dollars in wealth having evaporated in just two years, people were beginning to question capitalism. This was the moment that the consumer was starting to take back control and demand total transparency.

Gerzema predicted that brands would be forced to build longer-lasting products and create better, more intuitive customer service. He also said technology would enable us to connect with companies that share the values that we share. A decade later, Nancy Rademaker revealed that every single company now had got a new boss:

the customer. In her talk, Rademaker shows how we, as self-centered and on-demand customers require companies to deliver exceptional customer experiences. If they don't, they become obsolete. Elsewhere, Dr. Gerry Power talks about how he believes that ideas and creativity are the lifeblood of society.

Trust, privacy, and transparency are becoming the new currency. Insight, innovation, and change are now becoming impossible for brands and businesses of all sizes to ignore. Content is no longer king; it's providing customers with value that will help you win the hearts and minds of your audience.

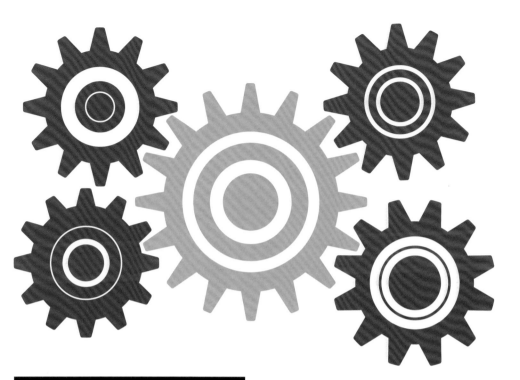

🔍 FIND OUT MORE

John Gerzema's talk:
"The Post-Crisis Consumer"
2009

· ·

Also try Nancy Rademaker's talk:
"Power to the Customer!"
2018

· ·

Gerry Power's talk:
"Insight, Innovation, Change:
Considerations from the Field"
2017

" DON'T FIND CUSTOMERS FOR YOUR PRODUCTS, FIND PRODUCTS FOR YOUR CUSTOMERS.

SETH GODIN, AUTHOR AND FORMER DOT-COM BUSINESS EXECUTIVE "

A POSITIVE FROM A NEGATIVE

Seek ways to turn your customers' biggest frustrations into your greatest opportunities.

On my podcast, I have interviewed more than one thousand guests that consist of CEOs, tech leaders, and start-up founders. In that time, all of them have shared one thing in common, when each encounters a problem, he or she creates a solution to fix it.

In her talk, Cofounder & CEO of CoDesign Factory Aya Jaff proves that some of the best business ideas are born when you are feeling angry. Jaff shares her story of turning anger into something highly essential for your progress in work and life. Johnny Rotten of the Sex Pistols famously sang that anger is an energy; maybe he was right all along.

It was the raw emotion of anger that gave Jaff the inspiration that no book, professor, or teacher ever could. It stopped her from sitting on a couch watching Netflix and inspired her to start coding her own solutions to the problems she encountered. It was also the inspiration for her book, *Moneymakers*.

When most of us encounter such an issue, we might be tempted to vent our frustration on a social media post. That's probably what your customers are doing right now. But are you listening to them?

Knowing what frustrates your customers and creating an innovative solution should be your next move.

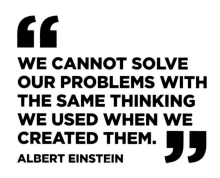

> **WE CANNOT SOLVE OUR PROBLEMS WITH THE SAME THINKING WE USED WHEN WE CREATED THEM.**
> **ALBERT EINSTEIN**

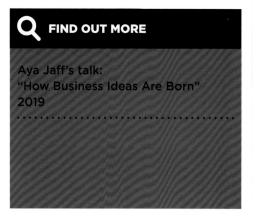

FIND OUT MORE

Aya Jaff's talk:
"How Business Ideas Are Born"
2019

DON'T BE AFRAID TO BREAK THE RULES

Having too many rules stifles innovation.

Back in 1997 when Apple was seen to be at the forefront of innovation, a commercial narrated by Steve Jobs saluted those that see the world differently despite being labeled the round pegs in the square holes that are not fond of rules. Ironically, as the ad pointed out, those that think they can change the world are the ones who usually do. This chapter explores how your internal "agitators" and "rabble-rousers" are your secret weapons as the experience economy continues to gather pace.

RULES ARE FOR FOOLS

Start by acknowledging that too many rules, processes, and metrics can hold you back.

Nobel Prize-winning economist Paul Krugman once famously wrote: "Productivity is not everything, but in the long run, it is almost everything." These were the powerful words that senior partner at The Boston Consulting Group Yves Morieux used to open his talk.

Morieux argues that many rules in the workplace have now become counterproductive to getting things done. "Take the holy trinity of efficiency: clarity, measurement, accountability. They make human efforts derail." Is your organization wasting human intelligence and working against the efforts of your staff? "When people don't cooperate, don't blame their mind-sets, their mentalities, or their

personality," Morieux enthuses. "Look at the work situations. Is it really in their interest to cooperate or not, if, when they cooperate, they are individually worse off? Why would they cooperate?"

When we blame personalities instead of the clarity, the accountability, or the measurement, we add injustice to ineffectiveness. Contrary to popular opinion, the best team is not the one with the most talented employees. It's the one in which members collaborate and cooperate with each other to achieve a common goal (see page 32). Sometimes that might mean breaking a few rules, but getting things done is the fortune awaiting the brave.

> **AS LEADERS, AS MANAGERS, ARE YOU MAKING IT INDIVIDUALLY USEFUL FOR PEOPLE TO COOPERATE? THE FUTURE OF OUR ORGANIZATIONS, COMPANIES, AND SOCIETIES HINGES ON YOUR ANSWER TO THESE QUESTIONS.**
> **YVES MORIEUX**

FIND OUT MORE

Yves Morieux's talk: "How Too Many Rules at Work Keep You From Getting Things Done" 2015

NO STRANGER TO INNOVATION

From an early age, we are taught not to talk to strangers. It's time to break that rule.

Despite what the twenty-four-hour news cycle tells us, most strangers aren't dangerous. We're uneasy around them because we have no context. We don't know what their intentions are. In her talk, stranger enthusiast Kio Stark explains how we should rely more on our senses, and not our fears, when meeting new people.

It's well documented that people often feel more comfortable talking honestly and openly about their inner selves when talking with strangers than they do with their friends and their families. We communicate better with strangers because interactions are often fleeting and without consequences, so we let our guard down.

According to Stark, we have a bias when it comes to people we're close to. "We expect them to understand us. We assume they do, and we expect them to read our minds." When attempting to innovate with colleagues, a combination of these biases and shared views can prevent any form of creativity.

Stark closes her talk with a few thought-provoking ideas. "We spend a lot of time teaching our children about strangers. What would happen if we spent more time teaching ourselves? We could reject all the ideas that make us so suspicious of each other. We could make a space for change."

So, what will you do differently to make space for change and encourage a different way of thinking within your own organization?

> **WHEN YOU TALK TO STRANGERS, YOU'RE MAKING BEAUTIFUL INTERRUPTIONS INTO THE EXPECTED NARRATIVE OF YOUR DAILY LIFE— AND THEIRS.**
> **KIO STARK**

🔍 FIND OUT MORE

Kio Stark's talk:
"Why You Should Talk to Strangers"
2011

A NEW CORPORATE DEMOCRACY

If you need proof that you can run a company with (almost) no rules, look no further.

 In his talk, CEO Ricardo Semler of Brazilian firm Semco Partners shares how he knows more than most about the challenges of running a complicated company that handles thousands of employees, hundreds of millions of dollars of business that makes rocket fuel propellant systems, and runs four thousand ATMs in Brazil. But how could they set their employees free from the traditional rules in the workplace?

What if they removed all of the boarding school aspects of work? Semler set out to create a radical form of corporate democracy, rethinking everything from meetings to how workers report their vacation days. By rewarding the wisdom of workers, he also set out to prove that a better work-life balance is not a myth.

The question he began asking was, "How do you set up for wisdom? We've come from the age of industrial revolution, an age of information, an age of knowledge, but we're not any closer to the age of wisdom." Many of the rules we have in place contradict our desire for innovation and a more collaborative environment.

Semler's solution may appear radical, but he is tackling the bigger questions. Simon Sinek also offers a timely reminder in his talks and advises "People don't buy what you do; they buy why you do it. And what you do simply proves what you believe." The only question that remains is: how do we design, and how do we organize for more wisdom?

Q FIND OUT MORE

Ricardo Semler's talk:
"How to Run a Company with (Almost) No Rules"
2015
. . . .
Also try Simon Sinek's talks on leadership

"

IF YOU HIRE PEOPLE JUST BECAUSE THEY CAN DO A JOB, THEY'LL WORK FOR YOUR MONEY. BUT IF YOU HIRE PEOPLE WHO BELIEVE WHAT YOU BELIEVE, THEY'LL WORK FOR YOU WITH BLOOD AND SWEAT AND TEARS. "

SIMON SINEK

FRUGAL INNOVATION

These three innovation principles will enable you to do more with less.

> **FRUGAL INNOVATION IS THE ABILITY TO CREATE MORE ECONOMIC AND SOCIAL VALUE USING FEWER RESOURCES. FRUGAL INNOVATION IS NOT ABOUT MAKING DO; IT'S ABOUT MAKING THINGS BETTER.**
>
> **NAVI RADJOU**

 In the twenty-first century, there is a long list of household names such as Blackberry, Nokia, and Blockbuster Video who failed to innovate. We all know how their stories ended. Before you celebrate being ahead of the curve, remember that real innovation is not something that you can throw money at, and the rules of the game have changed.

Many leaders believe that they cannot afford to innovate. But this is a myth. Innovation and leadership adviser Navi

Radjou spent years studying "jugaad," also known as frugal innovation. The practice was originally pioneered by entrepreneurs in emerging markets who didn't have the luxury of bottomless R&D budgets. In his talk, Radjou shares three principles that enable everyone to do more with less.

The first is to keep it simple. Don't be tempted to create solutions to impress customers. Your job is to make them easy enough to use and be widely accessible. Radjou's second principle is do not fall into the trap of trying to reinvent the

wheel. Innovation is about leveraging existing resources and assets that are widely available.

Finally, the third principle is to think and act horizontally rather than vertically. Remember, the most successful businesses are not the ones with the biggest budgets; they're the most innovative.

Q FIND OUT MORE

Navi Radjou's talk:
"Creative Problem-Solving in the Face of Extreme Limits"
2015

INNOVATIVE DECISION-MAKING

Remember to nurture a collaborative and inclusive environment.

 One of the problems in making decisions in groups is that it won't always go the way that you planned. Exploring how we interact with each other to reach decisions, neuroscientist Mariano Sigman and his colleague, professor of psychology and behavioral economics Dan Ariely, performed experiments with live crowds around the world. The results were revealed in a talk given by Sigman.

The pair discovered that just as one person is convinced that a certain behavior is completely wrong, someone sitting nearby firmly believes that it's completely right. It highlighted how diverse we humans are when it comes to morality.

It wasn't too surprising to discover that people with extreme opinions were more confident in their answers. By contrast, those who respond closer to the middle are often unsure of whether something is right or wrong, so their confidence level is lower.

"We are living in a time when the world's problems are more complex, and people are more polarized. Using science to help us understand how we interact and make decisions will hopefully spark interesting new ways to construct a better democracy."

Innovative decision-making is a challenge that you will encounter sooner rather than later. But a combination of the right people, processes, and a dash of science should keep on you on the right path to success.

Q FIND OUT MORE

Mariano Sigman's talk:
"How Can Groups Make Good Decisions?"
2017

GOOD COLLECTIVE DECISIONS REQUIRE TWO COMPONENTS: DELIBERATION AND DIVERSITY OF OPINIONS.
MARIANO SIGMAN

SMART FAILURE

It's time to rewrite the rule book around failure.

Innovation is changing the business landscape at breakneck speed. Creative output cannot keep up, and you will need to overcome a series of challenges and your fear of failure to succeed. In his talk, Eddie Obeng highlights a few significant changes and encourages everyone to embrace a culture of "smart failure."

Obeng highlights the contradictions in the workplace when it comes to innovation. Sure, every CEO says they want to see a culture of innovation and for employees to be empowered to be creative and take risks. Unfortunately, these words can get transformed as they travel through the air.

What they hear is, "Do crazy things, and then I'll fire you." Why? Because in the old world, getting stuff wrong was unacceptable. Obeng advises that we need to remove the mind-set that getting something wrong means you have failed. If you're doing something new, that nobody has ever done before, and you get it completely wrong, it's called smart failure.

Since this 2012 talk, agile companies are increasingly repeating the fail fast, and fail often mantra. Why? Failure can bring innovation and enable organizations to innovate faster. Maybe smart failure will help your company thrive in a fast-changing world.

> **WE SOLVE LAST YEAR'S PROBLEMS WITHOUT THINKING ABOUT THE FUTURE. IF YOU TRY AND THINK ABOUT IT, THE THINGS YOU'RE SOLVING NOW, WHAT PROBLEMS ARE THEY GOING TO BRING IN THE FUTURE?**
> **EDDIE OBENG**

🔍 FIND OUT MORE

Eddie Obeng's talk:
"Smart Failure for a Fast-Changing World"
2012

THE NEW RULES OF INNOVATION

Innovation? I do not think it means what you think it means . . .

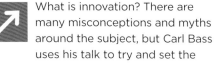 What is innovation? There are many misconceptions and myths around the subject, but Carl Bass uses his talk to try and set the record straight. "Innovation is the process by which we change the world. It's about making things better, in significant and hopefully meaningful ways."

As many of you reading this will know, innovation is hard. It requires taking chances and challenging those things we think we know with certainty. By its very nature innovation will also reward risk-taking and rule-breaking, both of which are not areas that you associate with successful organizations.

Tech trends highlight how the rules of the game have already changed. We no longer own products, we subscribe to experiences. The cloud is changing how we do business, and digital fabrication enables almost anything to be created by tech.

We can access information across a myriad of devices, and infinite computing means we can obtain an almost limitless volume of computer resources. Innovation will not stand still, and old rules or ways of working are no longer relevant. It's not just the rules that have changed, but the game of innovation itself.

> **THOSE WHO MAKE NEW INNOVATIONS AND ARE SUCCESSFUL IN BREAKING THE RULES ARE CREATING THE NEW RULES. AND IN A NEVER-ENDING CYCLE, THOSE NEW RULES WILL HAVE TO BE BROKEN AS WELL.**
> **CARL BASS**

Q FIND OUT MORE

Carl Bass's talk:
"The New Rules of Innovation"
2012

48/100

DON'T JUST BREAK THE RULES, CREATE NEW ONES

It is essential that you meaningfully connect with your community.

Community-engaged digital entrepreneur Kyle Gundrum delivered a few home truths in his talk about our social skills, or should I say lack of them. We have all heard personal and professional introductions that go something like "Hi, my name is . . . and my role is . . .." Kyle argues that it's boring. It is not unique, and it's not interesting. We basically reiterate things about ourselves that others can find out about us on our LinkedIn profiles or our resumes.

Although we are living in a hyperconnected world, we're not actually connecting and don't even talk to people in public. Gundrum believes that we need to rewrite the social rule book. He also asks, "Are you uplifting the community with your interactions? Are you a social catalyst? How could you be more of one? Do you feel connected to the community? And are you building the community?"

Echoing thoughts expressed by Kio Stark (see page 83), Kyle advises that, by starting to have more meaningful conversations, you are not actually breaking the rules. You are creating new ones that say; it's okay to talk to people in public, instead of scrolling aimlessly down your smartphone.

Intersecting with someone is not just a relationship opportunity. If you are looking for new business ideas, different points of view, or how to innovate more effectively—make a new rule to start talking to strangers.

Q FIND OUT MORE

Kyle Gundrum talk:
"Break the Rules: Be a Social Catalyst"
2015

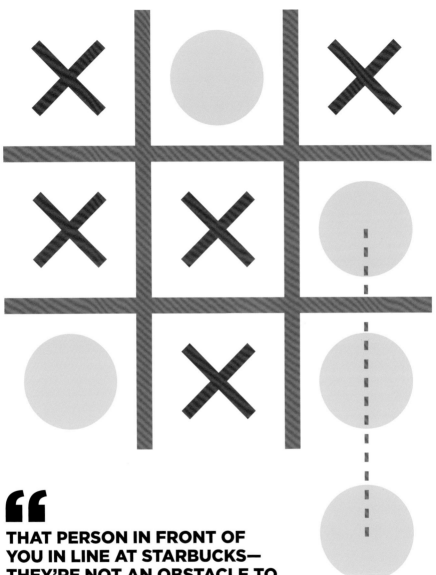

" THAT PERSON IN FRONT OF YOU IN LINE AT STARBUCKS— THEY'RE NOT AN OBSTACLE TO YOUR COFFEE, THEY'RE A RELATIONSHIP OPPORTUNITY. "

KYLE GUNDRUM

MAKING MEAT FROM PLANTS

What can you learn from organizations seeking to break the rules on a global level?

 The rules around the ways in which we think, innovate, and work differently extend beyond the work environment. We are also beginning to think about our social responsibilities and taking greater care of the planet on which we all reside. For example, conventional meat production causes harm to our environment and also presents risks to global health.

In 2019, humanity received a warning. Thirty of the world's leading scientists released the results of a three-year study into global agriculture and declared that meat production is destroying our planet and jeopardizing global health. But what is the answer?

In his 2019 talk, Bruce Friedrich delivers an alternative. "Let's grow meat from plants. Instead of growing plants, feeding them to animals, and increasing inefficiency, let's grow those plants, let's biomimic meat with them, let's make plant-based meat."

In a talk given in Copenhagen, futurist Angela Oguntala also urged the global community to reach further and push for real innovation and explore lab-grown food. She also argues that we need to be thinking about alternative futures and create plans for how to reach those desired futures.

Q FIND OUT MORE

Bruce Friedrich's talk:
"The Next Global Agricultural Revolution"
2019

Also try Angela Oguntala's talk:
"Reimagine the Future"
2016

"

INNOVATION HAS MORE THAN DOUBLED OUR LIFE SPAN, GIVEN US CHEAP ENERGY, AND MORE FOOD. IF WE PROJECT WHAT THE WORLD WILL BE LIKE TEN YEARS FROM NOW WITHOUT CONTINUING INNOVATION IN HEALTH, ENERGY, OR FOOD, THE PICTURE IS DARK. "

BILL GATES

REDEFINING HOW WE CARE

If you are looking for inspiration, see how new ways of thinking changed end-of-life care in the Netherlands.

Hogeweyk is a neighborhood in a small town very near Amsterdam, in the Netherlands. There is a mall with a restaurant, a pub, a superstore, and a clubroom. There are streets, alleys, and there's a theater. It is actually a nursing home for people who live with advanced dementia and that need 24–7 care and support.

Dementia is a terrible disease that affects the brain. Those affected lose concept of time, what's going on, and who people are. They're very confused. And because of that confusion, they get to be anxious, depressed, and aggressive.

Yvonne van Amerongen helped develop this groundbreaking Hogeweyk dementia care center in Amsterdam twenty-five years ago. The answer seems obvious now, and this different way of thinking has transformed how we approach care.

In her talk, van Amerongen advised that it's about: "looking at the person in front of you and looking at what does this person need now. And it's about a smile, it's about thinking different, it's about how you act, and that costs nothing."

In another talk, physician Timothy Ihrig provides a different approach to palliative care that prioritizes a patient's personal values. "This conversation is not about dying. It is about living. Living based on our values, what we find sacred, and how we want to write the chapters of our lives."

Q FIND OUT MORE

Yvonne van Amerongen's talk: "The 'Dementia Village' That's Redefining Elder Care" 2018

Also try Timothy Ihrig's talk: "What We Can Do to Die Well" 2013

"

HOW WOULD YOU PREFER TO SPEND THE LAST YEARS OF YOUR LIFE: IN A STERILE, HOSPITAL-LIKE INSTITUTION OR IN A VILLAGE WHERE EVERYTHING YOU KNOW, AND LOVE IS WITHIN WALKING DISTANCE? "

YVONNE VAN AMERONGEN

PREDICT THE FUTURE BY INVENTING IT

Discover new ways to fuel innovation in
your organization.

Are you looking to transform your corporate
culture and enable all those with the ability
to fuel innovation in your organization? This
chapter is aimed at helping you overcome any
creative challenges and learn from the mistakes
and successes of those who have already
navigated these uncharted digital waters.
Prepare to challenge your assumptions
and learn how you can create a culture of
innovation and strategy to help you prioritize
your best ideas.

EXPLORE THE WEIRD AND UNKNOWN

You should constantly be on the lookout for new ways to step outside of your comfort zone.

↗ As already discussed, we often surround ourselves with people who share our belief system (see page 68). Although this results in lovely conversations, anything you create will be a rehash of what you already know. To achieve the discovery and inspiration that we crave, we need to step out of our comfort zone.

Ironically, social media enables us to connect with everyone, but also to remove anyone or anything that doesn't share our worldview. But it's talking to those outside of our circle of trust that delivers new perceptions and understandings.

In her talk, computer engineer Maria Bezaitis highlights how, from a young age, we are conditioned by phrases such as "Stay away from anyone who's not familiar to you. Stick with the people you know. Stick with people like you." But the successes of Uber and Airbnb are proof that life is not like that.

Our social relations are increasingly mediated by data. We rely on technology to bring us a sense of discovery, a sense of surprise, and unpredictability. But it often delivers more of the same. We need to embrace strangers and strangeness.

After all, what interesting questions or exciting discoveries lie ahead for you in a world where you replace strangeness with what you have always known?

🔍 FIND OUT MORE

Maria Bezaitis's talk:
"Why We Need Strangeness"
2013
. . . .

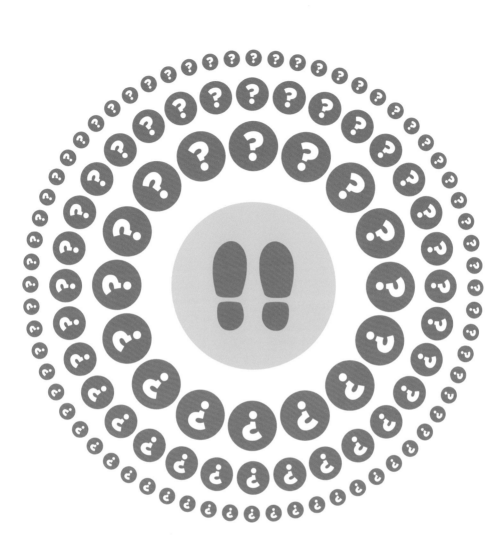

IN THE CONTEXT OF THIS BROAD RANGE OF DIGITAL RELATIONS, SAFELY SEEKING STRANGENESS MIGHT VERY WELL BE A NEW BASIS FOR INNOVATION.

MARIA BEZAITIS

THE CULTURE FACTOR

Take steps to replace the competitive pecking order.

> ## IT IS ONLY WHEN WE ACCEPT THAT EVERYBODY HAS VALUE THAT WE WILL LIBERATE THE ENERGY AND IMAGINATION AND MOMENTUM WE NEED TO CREATE THE BEST BEYOND MEASURE.
> **MARGARET HEFFERNAN**

Don't be fooled into thinking that business leaders are heroic soloists with a golden touch.

In her talk, business leader Margaret Heffernan delivers the wake-up call that "Companies don't have ideas; only people do." What motivates employees? The bonds, loyalty, and trust they develop with each other. In a nutshell, the mortar is equally as important as the bricks.

Many organizations are guilty of promoting "the super chicken model," where star employees are put on pedestals. But the talk reveals how this method does not deliver high-achieving teams. Heffernan argues that we need a new narrative and a radical rethink of what drives organizations to succeed and what it means to be a leader in a digital age.

Heffernan recalls how, in Sweden, some companies banned coffee cups at employees' desks because they wanted to encourage people to hang out and talk to each other around the coffee machines. In Maine, USA, a company called Idexx created vegetable gardens on campus so

that people from different parts of the business could work together.

Embedding a culture of innovation, and getting the most from your people requires a different approach. Breaking down the hierarchies from our analog past is the best way to enable teams to build a digital future together (see page 162).

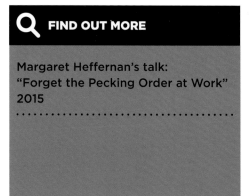

Q FIND OUT MORE

Margaret Heffernan's talk:
"Forget the Pecking Order at Work"
2015
· ·

WALK THE TALK

Break out of the meeting room in your quest to innovate.

The enhancing of performances through energized innovation sounds great on paper or in a strategy meeting. The reality is that we now spend more time sitting down each day than we do sleeping. How could we possibly expect to have boundless measures of enthusiasm when sitting in a fluorescent-lit meeting room looking at slides?

If you are serious about out-of-the-box thinking (see page 12), you will literally have to get outside of your box. Business innovator Nilofer Merchant decided to change a few unwritten rules and leave the meeting room behind to embark on hundreds of "walk the talk" meetings. But, what did she learn from the experience?

In her talk, Merchant states, "If we're going to solve problems and look at the world differently, maybe we can think about how to reframe these problems." The simple, walk-and-talk idea naturally enabled everything to become doable, sustainable, and viable.

Walking meetings can play a significant role in ensuring you are more focused, energetic, and creative than in traditional meeting environments. Possibly most important of all, they also give you some much-needed respite from interruptions, too.

> **WALK THE TALK. YOU'LL BE SURPRISED AT HOW FRESH AIR DRIVES FRESH THINKING, AND IN THE WAY THAT YOU DO, YOU'LL BRING INTO YOUR LIFE AN ENTIRELY NEW SET OF IDEAS.**
> **NILOFER MERCHANT**

Q FIND OUT MORE

Nilofer Merchant's talk: "Got a Meeting? Take a Walk" 2013

BEING HUMAN IN A DIGITAL WORLD

You should avoid any tendency to value the sciences any more than we value the humanities.

How do you build a team of innovative problem-solvers? Many of the titles in the long list of innovation rule books focus on addressing the STEM skills shortage, diversity, and introducing innovative technology. But in his talk, cofounder of IBM's Bluewolf, Eric Berridge advises that we should value the humanities just as much as the sciences.

Berridge also argues that people with backgrounds in the arts and humanities could bring creativity and insight to technical workplaces. Most people reading this will have witnessed the technologist struggling to communicate in the business world. The end-user and the business frequently fail to articulate their needs, too.

The way of doing things is holding us back from communicating and inventing together. Sure, sciences teach us how to build things. But it's the humanities that teach us what to build and why to build. Maybe we should try putting them on equal footing with the sciences. Why?

Berridge believes these different rules will "Teach us how to think critically. They are purposely unstructured, while the sciences are purposely structured. They teach us to persuade, and they give us our language, which we use to convert our emotions to thought and action." Let's get back to being human.

> **DIVERSITY SHOULDN'T END WITH GENDER OR RACE. WE NEED A DIVERSITY OF BACKGROUNDS AND SKILLS, WITH INTROVERTS AND EXTROVERTS, AND LEADERS AND FOLLOWERS.**
> **ERIC BERRIDGE**

Q FIND OUT MORE

Eric Berridge's talk:
"Why Tech Needs the Humanities"
2018

TAKE RISKS

Increase your luck by venturing outside of the safe zone.

Luck is defined as success or failure caused by chance (see page 11). Educator Tina Seelig became fascinated by the subject and quickly learned that luck is rarely a lightning strike. In her talk, she reveals that "it's much more like the wind, blowing constantly."

Luck is not just about being aware of opportunities around you and taking advantage of them either. "You need to understand that everyone who helps you on your journey is playing a huge role in getting you to your goals. And if you don't show appreciation, not only are you not closing the loop, but you're missing an opportunity."

Being brave enough to take calculated risks will also help you to catch the winds of luck in your sails, too. Increasing your luck is going to require a new set of rules, stepping out of your comfort zone, and facing your fears. Explorers who bravely navigate uncharted digital waters will be the ones that discover and seize opportunities that come their way.

It's easy to perceive the innovative brands that surround us as lucky. But we need to remember that they all began with a sales pitch and somebody replying, "That's crazy, it will never work."

Q FIND OUT MORE

Tina Seelig's talk:
"The Little Risks You Can Take to Increase Your Luck"
2018

" FIRST, YOU NEED TO TAKE SOME RISKS AND GET OUT OF YOUR COMFORT ZONE. SECOND, YOU NEED TO SHOW APPRECIATION. AND THIRD, YOU WANT TO CHANGE YOUR RELATIONSHIP WITH IDEAS. **"**

TINA SEELIG

THE RULE OF OPPORTUNITY

Creating a whole team of opportunity makers could help you innovate at scale.

Retiring the business rules of our past is long overdue, but we also need to create a new set of standards to live and work by. Author and columnist Kare Anderson asks us to reimagine the world and see one in which we all become greater opportunity makers, "with and for others."

In her talk, Anderson asks the audience to consider what kind of opportunity makers we might become? It's not about wealth, fancy titles, or a full address book. She advises that we should connect around each other's better side and bring it out.

Anderson also busts a few myths and disproves the if you're the smartest person in the room, you're in the wrong room theory. "The reality is that every one of us is better than anybody else at something," she enthuses. But when you connect with people around a shared interest and action, you're accustomed to serendipitous things happening into the future.

For those who believe we need more scale, not more innovation, Kare argues, we can do both. She advises, "We open ourselves up to those opportunities. In this room, there are key players in technology, key players who are uniquely positioned to scale systems and projects together."

Q FIND OUT MORE

Kare Anderson's talk:
"Be an Opportunity Maker"
2014
. . . .

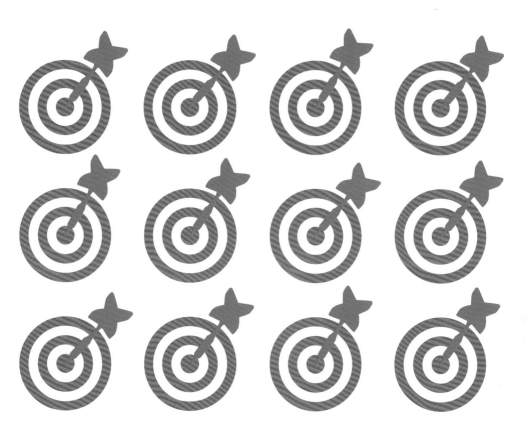

"OPPORTUNITY MAKERS KEEP HONING THEIR TOP STRENGTH, AND THEY BECOME PATTERN SEEKERS. THEY GET INVOLVED IN DIFFERENT WORLDS THAN THEIR WORLDS; THEY COMMUNICATE TO CONNECT AROUND SWEET SPOTS OF SHARED INTEREST."

KARE ANDERSON

SETTING THE RIGHT GOALS

Choosing the right objectives can mean the difference between success and failure.

Throughout his career, venture capitalist John Doerr has worked with many talented teams. Some have chosen the right objectives, and others found themselves distracted and chased the wrong ones. Predictably, some succeeded while others failed. But in his talk, Doerr shares what really makes a difference and the importance of setting the right goals for the right reasons.

He advises, "Objectives and Key Results, or OKRs, are a simple goal-setting system, and they work for organizations, they work for teams, they even work for individuals." Essentially, the objectives represent what you want to accomplish. The key results are how you're going to get that done.

The problem occurs when a business sets the wrong goals. Often, they lack the sense of purpose needed to inspire their teams. Do you have the right metrics in place? Have you written down your objectives and your key results?

At the start of your transformational journey, remember you cannot improve what you don't measure. But if you measure what really matters, you can avoid making unnecessary mistakes.

> **YOU MUST ANSWER THE QUESTION, 'WHY?' WHY? BECAUSE TRULY TRANSFORMATIONAL TEAMS COMBINE THEIR AMBITIONS TO THEIR PASSIONS, AND THEY DEVELOP A CLEAR AND COMPELLING SENSE OF WHY.**
> **JOHN DOERR**

Q FIND OUT MORE

John Doerr's talk:
"Why the Secret to Success Is Setting the Right Goals"
2018

THE ANTIDOTE TO APATHY

Don't let the apathy disease destroy your dreams of innovation.

When attempting to change the culture within an organization and fuel innovation, it's easy to become disheartened. It can feel as if people don't care and are not interested in making a difference. Professional rabble-rouser Dave Meslin believes that what we perceive as apathy is much more complicated.

In his talk, Meslin delivers a poignant message for business leaders on why their transformation efforts are failing. He delivers a wake-up call to those who have become entangled in a complex web of cultural barriers that reinforce disengagement. Think about it. How many of your employees have walked out of a meeting believing they can make a difference and submitted their ideas only to be blocked by obstacles? Disengagement usually follows as they walk away thinking, "What's the point, nothing ever changes."

Meslin tackles these problems head on and urges his audience to redefine apathy, not as some kind of internal syndrome, but as a complex web of obstacles. "If we can clearly define and identify what those obstacles are, then we can work together collectively to dismantle those obstacles."

Learning from these lessons will ensure that your initiative succeeds.

> **WE LIVE IN A WORLD THAT ACTIVELY DISCOURAGES ENGAGEMENT BY CONSTANTLY PUTTING OBSTACLES AND BARRIERS IN OUR WAY.**
> **DAVE MESLIN**

Q FIND OUT MORE

Dave Meslin's talk:
"The Antidote to Apathy"
2011

59/100
NO ROOM FOR EXCUSES

Learn how young Africans found a voice on Twitter.

 Businesses all over the world are desperately seeking ways to create viral content or marketing campaigns. Failed attempts at cleverness or trying too hard will make your business stand out for all the wrong reasons. Why do brands of all sizes still find it hard to be relevant and engaging to the audience that they serve?

Innovation can often occur in the purest and simple ways. For example, a young woman with an idea, an internet connection, and a sprinkle of creativity helped young Africans find a voice on Twitter. In her talk, Siyanda Mohutsiwa shares her story of discovering an innovative way to unite young African voices in Africa. A viral Tweet.

It is difficult not to be inspired by a group of young Africans that were bursting with creative energy and innovative ideas, and used them to overcome significant challenges. Mohutsiwa shares the African saying, "If you want to go fast, you go alone, but if you want to go far, you go together."

She believes that social Pan-Africanism is how they can go far together.

The internet is enabling an entire continent to think collaboratively and innovate together. Mohutsiwa has a vision that the days of saying "Well, this wouldn't work in my country" and then giving up will be eradicated once and for all. As a business leader, what is your vision?

Q FIND OUT MORE

Siyanda Mohutsiwa's talk:
"How Young Africans Found a Voice on Twitter"
2016

MY DREAM IS THAT YOUNG AFRICANS STOP ALLOWING BORDERS AND CIRCUMSTANCE TO SUFFOCATE OUR INNOVATION.

SIYANDA MOHUTSIWA

FOCUS ON TODAY

Stop worrying about the future and innovate in the present.

Innovating is exciting. But it is also incredibly easy to fall into the trap of getting overwhelmed with excitement. Having newsfeeds bombarded with emerging technologies such as 5G, AI, Machine Learning, and Blockchain doesn't help either. Rather than gazing into a crystal ball, entrepreneur Joi Ito urges us all to be a now-ist rather than a futurist.

It's easy to lose your way after being distracted by the next big thing. But Ito uses his talk to share the lessons that he has learned. "Create in the moment: build quickly and improve constantly, without waiting for permission or for proof that you have the right idea."

For those who frequently feel overwhelmed at the breakneck speed of change, Ito also has some reassuring advice. "Even though the world is extremely complex, what you need to do is very simple. I think it's about stopping this notion that you need to plan everything, and you need to be so prepared. Focus on being connected, always learning, fully aware, and super present."

Arika Shiga also advises how to master the art of living in the moment and how to make the necessary changes in her talk. But, remember the best way of predicting the future is to create it today.

Q FIND OUT MORE

Joi Ito's talk:
"Want to innovate? Become a 'Now-ist.'"
2014

....

Also try Arika Shiga's talk:
"The Art of Living in the Moment and Making the Necessary Changes"
2015

" I DON'T LIKE THE WORD 'FUTURIST.' I THINK WE SHOULD BE NOW-ISTS LIKE WE ARE RIGHT NOW. **"**

JOI ITO

REMEMBER, YOU NEVER FAIL. YOU LEARN.

Failure is an important part of innovation.

We all celebrate our successes online and are guilty of creating our own highlight reels on LinkedIn, Instagram, and Facebook. We proudly showcase ourselves accepting awards or celebrating our achievements. But we don't learn anything from our highs. It's the mistakes, missteps, and failures that offer the most value. So why are we so afraid of failure? This chapter explores how failure often leads to innovation.

FAILING MINDFULLY

Failure is not just an opportunity to learn.
It's a responsibility.

Leticia Gasca is the cofounder of the Failure Institute, the first think tank in the world devoted to studying business failure and the reasons behind it. Could it be time to reevaluate how we define and learn from failure?

It wasn't too long ago that failure was greeted with embarrassment and even shame. Some large organizations still rule by fear and punish those who fail. In her talk, Gasca warns that, "when we excessively punish those who fail, we stifle innovation and business creation, the engines of economic growth in any country."

By contrast, start-ups adopt a more radical fail-fast approach (see page 16). But maybe the answer is not in punishing failure or celebrating it as an opportunity. With an emphasis on failing mindfully, Gasca talks about the importance of being aware of the impact and consequences of failure.

Recognizing the lessons learned, and the responsibility to share those learnings with the world, could provide opportunities for others to innovate too. In another talk, the author of *Eat, Pray, Love*, Elizabeth Gilbert, reveals that by sharing our failures, weaknesses, and experiences, we can reduce trial and error of failure. But it doesn't have to define you.

> **YOU CAN MEASURE YOUR WORTH BY YOUR DEDICATION TO YOUR PATH, NOT BY YOUR SUCCESSES OR FAILURES.**
> **ELIZABETH GILBERT**

Q FIND OUT MORE

Leticia Gasca's talk:
"Don't Fail Fast—Fail Mindfully"
2018

Also try Elizabeth Gilbert's talk:
"Success, Failure, and the Drive to Keep Creating"
2014

KILL GROUPTHINK

The way forward is to be open to criticism and different points of view.

Umberto Callegari is known for his unconventional, creative thinking and is widely considered to be an innovator in the Internet of Things (IoT) and consulting community. In his talk, he dares to ask the questions: Why do so many businesses fail to innovate? And when we talk about a lack of innovation, do we label it as a shortage of creativity?

Contrary to popular opinion, innovation is not a stroke of genius. It's a process. The problem is that many large corporations rely on the existing paradigm that gave them their fortune in the first place. This ultimately leads to groupthink, where entire teams in search of harmony or conformity sleepwalk into the same irrational or dysfunctional decision-making.

Groupthink is the worst enemy of innovation. The only antidote is for us to immerse ourselves in different domains and explore diverse points of view. Callegari advises his audience to welcome criticism because it's only through criticism and radical collaboration that we can kill groupthink once and for all. Think about it: if you keep doing things the same way, you can't be too surprised if you keep getting the same results.

> **THE REASONABLE MAN ADAPTS HIMSELF TO THE WORLD: THE UNREASONABLE ONE PERSISTS IN TRYING TO ADAPT THE WORLD TO HIMSELF. THEREFORE, ALL PROGRESS DEPENDS ON THE UNREASONABLE MAN.**
> **GEORGE BERNARD SHAW, PLAYWRIGHT**

Q FIND OUT MORE

Umberto Callegari's talk: "Why Do We Fail to Innovate?" 2017

Also try Astro Teller's talk: "The Unexpected Benefit of Celebrating Failure" 2016

NEVER GIVE UP

Innovation requires passion and perseverance.

Many organizations naively think that success will flourish from purpose-built innovation labs with multicolored beanbags. The reality is that perseverance, hard work, and a constant drive to improve are the more realistic ingredients required to innovate.

Teaching seventh graders, Angela Lee Duckworth discovered that "grit" is a better indicator of success than factors such as IQ or family income, and the same is true in the workplace. In her talk, Duckworth advises that, "Grit is sticking with your future, day in, day out, not just for the week, not just for the month, but for years, and working really hard to make that future a reality. Grit is living life like it's a marathon, not a sprint." If you are serious about innovation, you need to be in it for the long haul and be willing to measure just how successful your efforts have been (see also Chapter 9).

Pioneering researcher in the field of motivation, Carol Dweck advises in her talk that wannabe innovators also need to adopt a "growth mind-set" to grow the brain's capacity to learn. Only by continuously learning and improving can you genuinely understand that innovation is a journey, not a destination.

FIND OUT MORE

Angela Lee Duckworth's talk:
"Grit: The Power of Passion and
Perseverance"
2013

. . . .

Also try Carol Dweck's talk:
"The Power of Believing That You
Can Improve"
2014

"
**WE HAVE TO BE
WILLING TO FAIL, TO
BE WRONG, TO START
OVER AGAIN WITH
LESSONS LEARNED. "**
ANGELA LEE DUCKWORTH

IT'S OK TO HAVE REGRETS

Living with being wrong can help you innovate.

From a young age, we are conditioned to believe that getting things wrong is foolish, and the only way to succeed in life is not to make any mistakes. We then spend the rest of our lives trying to avoid thinking about the horrifying possibility that we could be wrong.

Kathryn Schulz, author of *Being Wrong: Adventures in the Margin of Error*, performed not one, but two talks on the subject of regret and getting things wrong. Schulz advised everyone to step outside of the self-imposed limitations of rightness and have the courage to say: "I don't know. Maybe I'm wrong."

We somehow convince ourselves that getting something wrong means there's something wrong with us. So, we lock ourselves in echo chambers and end up believing that we are always right. Why? Schulz believes it's because it makes us feel smart and responsible and virtuous and safe. But all of these traits are natural enemies of innovation.

On the subject of regret, Schulz warns that throwing caution to the wind and making foolish decisions under the guise of living a life of no regrets is a bad idea. Sometimes we need to learn to live not without regret, but with it.

Q FIND OUT MORE

Kathryn Schulz's talks:
"On Being Wrong"
2011

"Don't Regret Regret"
2011

WE NEED TO LEARN TO LOVE THE FLAWED, IMPERFECT THINGS. REGRET DOESN'T REMIND US THAT WE DID BADLY. IT REMINDS US THAT WE KNOW WE CAN DO BETTER.

KATHRYN SCHULZ

HAVE NO FEAR

Removing fear from the innovation equation can make the impossible possible.

 What would you attempt to do if you knew you could not fail? This is a question that technology developer Regina Dugan asks the audience in her talk. She goes on to describe how, by eradicating the fear of failure, they would be able to bring extraordinary projects to life, such as a robotic hummingbird or a prosthetic arm controlled by thought.

Dugan also warns that we shouldn't over-romanticize or encourage failing, but we should actively discourage our fear of failure. Why? Because it's not failure itself that constrains us and prevents greater innovation or creativity. Rather, when fostering an innovative mind-set, you need to accept that failure will play a significant role in getting you to where you need to be. Fear of failure will prevent you from implementing anything. Maybe French prime minister Georges Clemenceau said it best when he advised: "Life gets interesting when we fail because it's a sign that we've surpassed ourselves."

In her talk Dugan showcases several examples of what happens when you remove fear from the equation. Often, impossible things suddenly become possible. Consider this message your wake-up call to set you and your teams free of their traditional fears.

Q FIND OUT MORE

Regina Dugan's talk:
"From Mach-20 Glider to Hummingbird Drone"
2012

Also try Richard Browning's talk:
"How I Built a Jet Suit"
2017

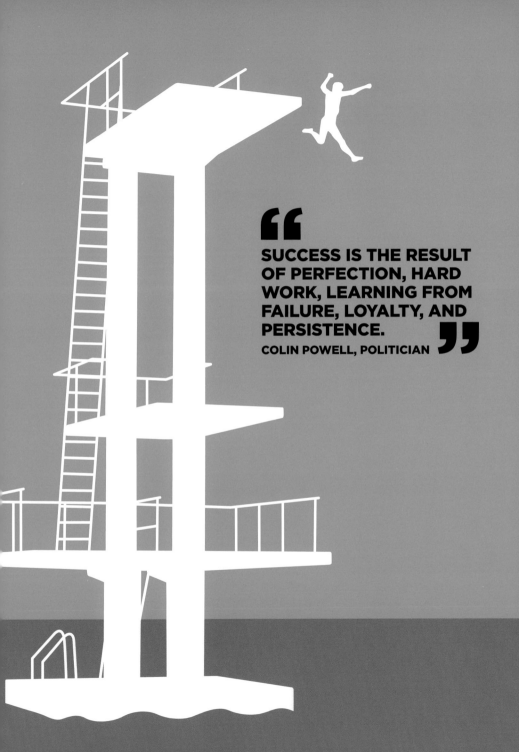

SUCCESS IS THE RESULT OF PERFECTION, HARD WORK, LEARNING FROM FAILURE, LOYALTY, AND PERSISTENCE.
COLIN POWELL, POLITICIAN

ADVERSITY CAN DRIVE INNOVATION

Always look for ways to transform adversity into opportunity.

Every person reading this book will face adversity during his or her lifetime. The problem is that many of us will also allow failures or challenges to hold us back. Maybe we should look at adversity differently and flip it to our advantage. For example, on your innovation journey, how many of your perceived barriers are real?

In her talk, founder and CEO of Customer Fanatix Heather Younger urges her audience to take control of adversity and make it work for themselves by embracing cognitive reframing—a psychological technique that can help anyone identify those dreaded irrational or maladaptive thoughts.

Younger explains how reframing can enable entire teams to view ideas, concepts, and emotions in a different light to help them discover more positive alternatives and therefore become more innovative as a result.

In another talk, innovation thought leader Larry Keeley talks about how Greece could innovate its way out of its, then current, time of great adversity. He explains that the most interesting and useful forms of innovation correlate more closely with resource scarcity, rather than resource abundance.

A SETBACK IS A SETUP FOR A COMEBACK.
T. D. JAKES, PASTOR

FIND OUT MORE

Heather Younger's talks: "Transforming Adversity into Opportunity" 2019

Also try Larry Keeley's talk "Flipping Adversity to Advantage" 2011

BOUNCING BACK

Resilience is key to gaining a new perspective.

Anyone who has seen footage of the Apollo 13 Moon Landing mission will recall Gene Kranz's phrase, "failure is not an option." However, in his research for NASA, psychotherapist Raphael Rose discovered that it is indeed an option.

In his talk, Rose advises that failure is required to promote resilience. Resilience means that you face your challenges head-on, which also helps you bounce back and recover. Rather than trying to avoid the problematic untrodden path, we should confront our fears of failure and explore the unknown (see page 124).

Rose finishes his talk by imploring each member of the audience to welcome stress, rise to the challenges in his or her life, and learn from mistakes. As you rebound from failure and build resilience, it will become much easier to innovate on the long road ahead.

In a talk by Leland Melvin, we get the opportunity to experience an astronaut's view of curiosity, perspective, and change. It was by accepting risks and seizing the opportunities that he found himself on the International Space Station.

> **WE EXPLORE, OR WE EXPIRE. THAT'S ABOUT IT.**
> **BUZZ ALDRIN**

FIND OUT MORE

Raphael Rose's talk:
"From Stress to Resilience"
2019

Also try Leland Melvin's talk:
"An Astronaut's Story of Curiosity, Perspective, and Change"
2019

NOBODY'S PERFECT

Overthinking an idea stifles innovation efforts.

Many businesses are crippled because they overthink almost everything. The result is often a severe case of analysis paralysis (see page 10). Replacing a culture of perfectionism with an environment that celebrates, rather than fears, imperfection can be challenging. But it is possible.

In her talk, recovering perfectionist and former pro runner Charly Haversat challenges our obsession with perfection and the unwillingness to compromise what it creates. While we continuously obsess about getting everything 100 percent right, she dares to ask, are we actually getting anything done?

However, Haversat passionately argues that businesses can stop the rot and get back on track. She advises, "Corporations can make a huge change by moving away from cultures of fear and moving toward cultures of innovation." But we need a change of mind-set both in and outside of the office.

In his talk, Thomas Curran speaks about our increasing obsession with attaining the perfect life and lifestyle. A new visual culture is promoting the use of highlight

" CONTINUOUS IMPROVEMENT IS BETTER THAN DELAYED PERFECTION. "

MARK TWAIN, AUTHOR

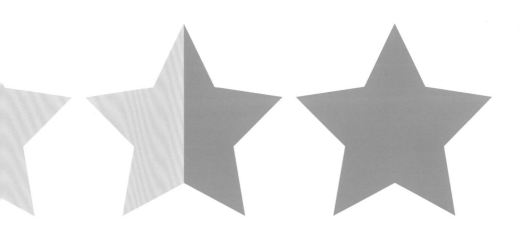

reels on platforms such as Instagram, Facebook, and Snapchat—the appearance of perfection has become more important than reality. Both talks explore how we should all invest more time in celebrating the joys and the beauties of imperfection.

🔍 **FIND OUT MORE**

Charly Haversat's talk:
"Perfectionism Holds Us Back.
Here's Why."
2015

Also try Thomas Curran's talk:
"Our Dangerous Obsession with
Perfectionism Is Getting Worse"
2019

EMBRACE NEAR WINS

Success forms just one part of the innovation story.

Innovation is a long journey of continuous improvement and not a destination. When approached the right way, it can also be a catalyst for culture change that can drive new business strategies. You will also need plenty of patience, time, and commitment to make it all work.

In a digital age of instant gratification, we celebrate creativity and mastery. Art historian Sarah Lewis discovered that success is just a moment and that we need to value the gift of those near wins that push us forward too. In her talk, Lewis explains how building on the unfinished ideas helps us succeed. Coming close to what you thought you wanted and not being afraid to pivot along the way will help you to exceed your expectations. After all, innovation is a journey that should never end.

One of the examples that Lewis uses in her talk is a conversation she had with the Arctic explorer Ben Saunders. She recalls how he told her that his triumphs were not the result of a grand achievement. It was the propulsion of a lineage of near wins. Lewis asks you to consider the role of the almost failures—the near wins—in your own life and business.

> **MASTERY IS IN THE REACHING, NOT IN THE ARRIVING. SO HOW DO YOU KEEP REACHING?**
> **SARAH LEWIS**

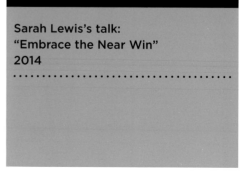

Q FIND OUT MORE

Sarah Lewis's talk:
"Embrace the Near Win"
2014

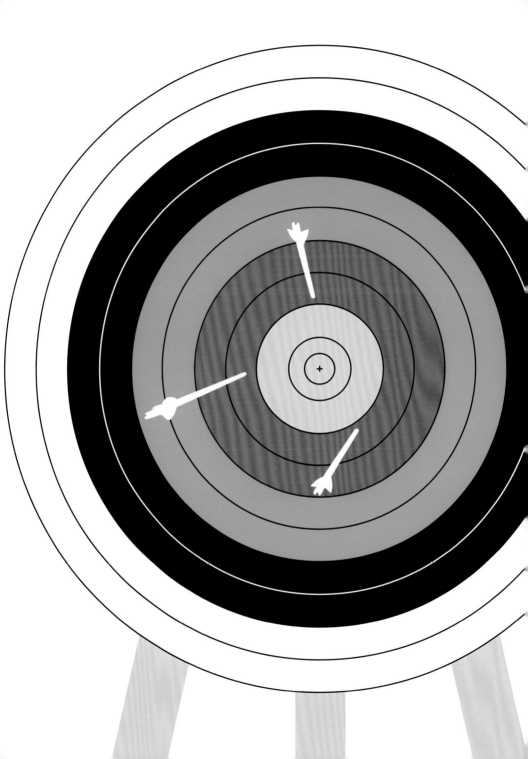

IS BIOLOGY THE SECRET TO BUSINESS SURVIVAL?

It is important not to forget how your brand became successful.

> **ADAPTABILITY AND CONSTANT INNOVATION ARE KEY TO THE SURVIVAL OF ANY COMPANY OPERATING IN A COMPETITIVE MARKET.**
> **SHIV NADAR, FOUNDER OF HCL TECHNOLOGIES**

Only fifty-four of the original companies remain on the Fortune 500 list since it was first released in 1955. In recent years, companies such as Nokia, Xerox, Yahoo, and JCPenney have presented perfect examples of what happens to brands that don't innovate. Increasingly paranoid brands are attempting to disrupt before they are disrupted.

However, Director of the BCG Henderson Institute Martin Reeves reveals in his talk that maybe these firms should be looking for inspiration within their own immune systems. Reeves shares a range of startling statistics about shrinking corporate life spans. He also offers hope by explaining how leaders can apply a range of principles from living organisms to build resilient businesses that can flourish in the face of change.

Reeves also highlights how every small entrepreneurial company will always act biologically. Why? Because they lack the resources to shape their environment through brute force. Ironically, every large company started in the same way, but perhaps many lose their ability to think and act biologically along their successful journey.

When looking at difference perspectives, leaders also need to look much closer to home. Large organizations must rejuvenate their ability to think biologically if they want to survive in a fast-moving digital age.

Q FIND OUT MORE

Martin Reeves's talk:
"How to Build a Business That Lasts 100 Years"
2016
. . . .

EMBRACE DIVERSITY OF THOUGHT

New ways of thinking can drive meaningful change.

Businesses across every industry all share one thing in common. They serve a diverse customer base. It's widely accepted that understanding your customers is crucial to the success of your business (see Chapter 4). It's only reasonable, therefore, to assume you will need a diverse set of employees. Their breadth of thought and willingness to explore new ways of thinking could be the secret to unlocking innovation in your organization.

WHY DIVERSITY?

Differing views offer new perspectives.

 Every workplace should reflect the population as a whole. How else can a business expect to serve its diverse range of customers? However, the importance of diversity of thought really shines through when teams attempt to innovate together.

In his talk, Kristian Ribberstrom of The Medici Group encourages everyone to move the diversity discourse beyond "doing the right thing" and quotas. Ribberstrom also believes that we have an opportunity for groundbreaking innovation when we tear down silos, cross boundaries, and purposefully learn from the unfamiliar, unknown, and unexpected.

Only those who have a lot of tools at their disposal will have insights around different perspectives. Diversity enables teams to look at problems from multiple angles. By contrast, homogeneous groups are not innovative. Sure, they work well as teams and can fix the same problem in the same way. But, coming up with creative ideas and executing them requires something entirely different.

In her talk, novelist Chimamanda Ngozi Adichie warns that if we only hear a single story about another person or country, we risk a misunderstanding. She also offers a timely reminder that our lives and cultures are composed of many overlapping stories, and with that comes big responsibility.

🔍 FIND OUT MORE

Kristian Ribberstrom's talk: "Using Diversity to Drive Innovation" 2013

Also try Chimamanda Ngozi Adichie's talk: "The Danger of a Single Story" 2009

WE NEED DIVERSITY OF THOUGHT IN THE WORLD TO FACE THE NEW CHALLENGES.

TIM BERNERS-LEE

CROSS-CULTURE COLLABORATION

In celebrating our differences we can learn from each other.

Although we all have instant and constant access to knowledge using our smart devices, we often forget to learn from each other. Li Chang, a Boeing engineer, used his talk to encourage the members of his audience to grow and expand beyond their comfort zone on a journey of collaborative innovation.

Chang offered a timely reminder that innovation starts with all of us. By celebrating our differences, there is an opportunity to collaborate to innovate and enrich our world. He also paints a picture of how a diverse thinking culture can also improve gap intelligence and integrate creative, constructive, and strategic thinking for greater innovation.

Novelist Elif Shafak echoes these sentiments in her talk about the revolutionary power of diverse thought. Only when we overcome our preconceived notions about people from different cultures and backgrounds can we begin to see our shared humanity and emotional experiences. Understanding that our thinking is shaped by our culture and background will be an obvious concept for most people to grasp. However, Shafak illustrates these points beautifully with words that you can almost taste.

> **DIVERSITY: THE ART OF THINKING INDEPENDENTLY TOGETHER.**
> **MALCOLM FORBES, ENTREPRENEUR**

Q FIND OUT MORE

Li Chang's talk:
"Drive Innovation Through Cognitive Diversity"
2017

Also try Elif Shafak's talk:
"The Revolutionary Power of Diverse Thought"
2017

MAKE SPACE IN THE WORKPLACE

It is time to bring people together in the name of progress.

Can you imagine a place where people of all colors and all races worked side by side, bringing their unassimilated, authentic selves to work every day? A workplace where the difference that they bring is both recognized and respected? In a candid talk, inclusion advocate Janet Stovall provides an inspiring narrative where we all work together to fix what's broken.

If organizations are serious about innovation, they need to be a part of the solution rather than the problem. "If you have customers, wouldn't it make sense if they looked a little bit like the people that work for you?"

As the experience economy gathers pace, companies need to leverage a diverse set of experiences, perspectives, and backgrounds to innovate and unlock new ideas. Diversity is the only way to channel different perspectives and new ways of thinking that foster innovation.

Leaders have a responsibility to bring people together in the name of progress. Stovall closes her talk by emploring everyone to work together to make it happen. We need to do more than just pray for change to happen. We need to start moving our feet to make it happen.

> **"**
> **DIVERSITY IS ABOUT ALL OF US, AND ABOUT US HAVING TO FIGURE OUT HOW TO WALK THROUGH THIS WORLD TOGETHER.**
> **JACQUELINE WOODSON, AUTHOR** **"**

🔍 FIND OUT MORE

Janet Stovall's talk:
"How to Get Serious About Diversity and Inclusion in the Workplace"
2018

OVERCOMING BIAS

Removing biases can improve personal growth.

> ## BIASES ARE THE STORIES WE MAKE UP ABOUT PEOPLE BEFORE WE KNOW WHO THEY ARE. BUT HOW ARE WE GOING TO KNOW WHO THEY ARE WHEN WE'VE BEEN TOLD TO AVOID AND BE AFRAID OF THEM?
>
> **VERNĀ MYERS**

We are living in a digital age dominated by social media newsfeeds where we surround ourselves with what we love and remove everything that we don't. Somewhere along the way, we have created echo chambers where our existing biases are exaggerated by reducing our exposure to other points of view.

How can we expect teams to innovate if some members are locked inside of bubbles with extremely narrow worldviews? In her talk, inclusion strategist Vernā Myers looks closely at prevailing subconscious attitudes and provides a timely warning of just how dangerous our unchecked biases can be.

Every business is desperately trying to generate the best ideas from its people across all levels of its organization. Innovation is not about finding someone with a creative spark. It's something that evolves with the personal growth of everyone involved. (For a wider discussion on effective leadership, see Chapter 2).

Building relationships with those that you may perceive to be different from you or have a different worldview is critical.

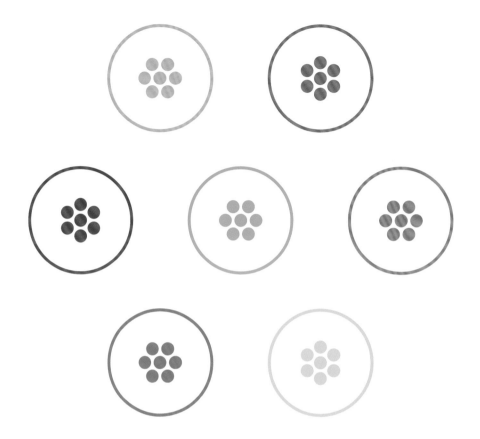

Seeking new perspectives will deliver personal growth that is crucial to making any innovation initiative a success.

Myers makes a simple plea to her audience and asks each member to acknowledge his or her biases. She also urges everyone to move toward, not away from, the groups that make them feel uncomfortable.

Q FIND OUT MORE

Vernā Myers' talk:
"How to Overcome Our Biases? Walk Boldly Toward Them"
2011
. . . .
Also try Thandie Newton's talk:
"Embracing Otherness, Embracing Myself"
2011

INCREASE YOUR SELF-AWARENESS

If you want to change the world, start with yourself.

Self-awareness is becoming increasingly important, both in and outside of the workplace.

It helps us shake off the shackles of sameness and explore complexity based on differences and diversity. In her talk, organizational psychologist Tasha Eurich reveals that, although we all like to think that we are self-aware, the reality is quite different.

After spending four years researching what being self-aware really means, Eurich made a surprising discovery about human perception. By embracing introspective thinking, there is a simple way that we can all get to know ourselves just a little bit better. Eurich discovered that we could increase our self-awareness with a straightforward fix. We just need to change one simple word—"why"—to "what." Eurich goes on to explain that, " 'Why' questions trap us in that rearview mirror. But 'what' questions move us forward to our future."

In William L. Sparks's talk, the professor of behavioral science illustrates the transformative potential of giving and receiving feedback. Although it can feel incredibly daunting, he talks about how feedback can also unlock the power of self-awareness.

As human beings, we can understand who we are, what we want to contribute, and the kind of life we want to lead. As with innovation, the quest for self-awareness never stops. Only you can choose how you grow as a person from your mistakes, experiences, and achievements. Dare you look at yourself in the mirror?

Q FIND OUT MORE

Tasha Eurich's talk:
"Increase Our Self-Awareness with One Simple Fix"
2017

Also try William L. Sparks' talk:
"The Power of Self-Awareness"
2018

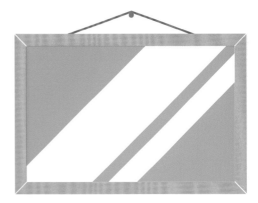

> # "
> ## YESTERDAY I WAS CLEVER, SO I WANTED TO CHANGE THE WORLD. TODAY I'M WISE, SO I AM CHANGING MYSELF.
> **RUMI, SUFI MYSTIC** "

LEARN BY EXAMPLE

It can take just one person to deliver meaningful change.

As a young designer, Emily Pilloton found herself becoming frustrated by the scarcity of meaningful work in the design world. She decided to take a new direction and make a difference through design-led community transformation.

A design-build class called Studio H was born. In her talk, Pilloton speaks about how she focused on uniting high schoolers' minds and bodies to deliver meaningful change. As a result, smart design was able to deliver new opportunities to the poorest county in her state.

As with innovation, design is a steady process of constant education. However, to reeducate ourselves and adopt a new way of thinking around the things that really matter, we have to step out of our comfort zone. When Pilloton shared her story of how thirteen students and two teachers made a difference, it also highlighted what can happen when we view the people around us as human beings.

This is just one instance of what can happen when you unite a diverse rural community. A new future was created for local education and maybe even for the future of design as we know it.

"
INNOVATION DOESN'T EQUAL SOCIAL GOOD, BUT SOCIAL GOOD CAN BE ACCELERATED BY INNOVATION PROVIDED THAT PURPOSE IS AT THE HEART OF THAT INNOVATION. "
ANONYMOUS

Q FIND OUT MORE

Emily Pilloton's talk:
"Teaching Design for Change"
2010

Also try Jeff Snell's talk:
"The Power of Social Innovation"
2014

MAKE A DIFFERENCE

Everyone must play a part in correcting diversity and inclusion.

Discrimination comes in many forms. Gender, race, ethnicity, religion, disability, and sexual orientation are just a handful of many factors that prevent some of us from thriving in a digital age. It could also grind your innovation efforts to a screaming halt.

In her talk, business innovator Melinda Epler delivers the truth that there's no magic wand for correcting diversity and inclusion. The reality is that change happens one person at a time, one act and one word at a time. But, each of us must learn to be an ally for those who face discrimination.

For a wider discussion on being an advocate for change, see Chapter 3. Epler advises that, "If companies can teach their people to be allies, diversity and inclusion programs are stronger."

In her closure, Epler also passionately speaks of how supporting one another enables us to thrive together. "When we thrive, we build better teams, better products, and better companies." Consider this your true calling to be a better ally in the workplace.

> ## PEACE IS NOT UNITY IN SIMILARITY BUT UNITY IN DIVERSITY, IN THE COMPARISON AND CONCILIATION OF DIFFERENCES.
> **MIKHAIL GORBACHEV, FORMER RUSSIAN PRESIDENT**

🔍 FIND OUT MORE

Melinda Epler's talk:
"Three Ways to Be a Better Ally in the Workplace"
2018

Also try Tom Wujec's talk:
"Build a Tower, Build a Team"
2014

78/100
TRUST AND TRANSPARENCY

A business needs to be transparent, inclusive, and accountable.

> **WHEN MAKING SALES, THE FIRST PEOPLE WHO WILL TRUST YOU WILL BE STRANGERS. FRIENDS WILL BE SHIELDING AGAINST YOU, AND FAIR-WEATHER FRIENDS WILL DISTANCE FROM YOU. FAMILY WILL LOOK DOWN UPON YOU.**
>
> **JACK MA, COFOUNDER OF THE ALIBABA GROUP**

Do you remember a time when we only placed our trust in governments, banks, and businesses? In recent years, our concept of trust has been transformed. We routinely check user reviews on Trip Advisor before booking a holiday and read consumer reviews on Amazon before we hit the one-click checkout button.

Author Rachel Botsman uses her talks to highlight how we are increasingly seeking the advice of strangers. Platforms such as Airbnb and Uber are thriving thanks to the technology that removes the need for intermediaries. As emerging technologies such as Blockchain begin to gather pace, Botsman believes that we could be entering a new era of trust and transparency.

Every day, five million people take a trust leap and ride with Uber. In China, on the ride-sharing platform Didi, eleven million rides are made each day. That's 127 rides per second, showing that this is a cross-cultural phenomenon. These are just two examples of how technology is creating trust between people on a scale never possible before.

It's easy to become distracted by the technical aspects of exponential change. But Botsman warns her audience that the real disruption isn't technological at all, it's the trust shift that it is creating. Businesses that embrace opportunities to design more transparent, inclusive, and accountable systems are the ones that will earn the trust of their future customers.

Q FIND OUT MORE

Rachel Botsman's talks:
"We've Stopped Trusting Institutions and Started Trusting Strangers"
2016
....
"The Currency of the New Economy Is Trust"
2012

THE CHANGE MONSTER

Diversity can help overcome the fear of change.

Creating an environment in which a business can harness the unique insights and experience of its employees is something that many leaders underestimate. Development expert Patrick Forth suggests that our love of technology is perhaps rivaled only by our fear of change in his talk.

However, the reality is that by 2020, an estimated 75 percent of the Fortune 500 will be names we've never heard of. The incredibly high failure rate serves as a wake-up call for large companies to innovate and embrace change if they are serious about thriving in a digital age.

Businesses are already becoming more adaptive, agile, and efficient. Forth also believes these changes could pave the way for a redefinition of exactly what competitive advantage means. Leaders must embrace culture change if they want to avoid becoming the next Blockbuster Video or Kodak. (For a wider discussion on the fear of change, see Chapter 3.)

In his closure, Forth provides a vision of what success and failure will look like in the not-so-distant future. Will you be able to change your organization's clock speed from linear to exponential? Or will you be devoured by the change monster? The rest is up to you.

In another talk, George Andriopoulos talks about disrupting the limits that organizations impose on themselves. He urges his audience to stop thinking about changing how the game is played and to create a brand new game instead.

FIND OUT MORE

Patrick Forth's talk:
"Technology Disruption Meets the Change Monster . . . Who Wins?"
2014

. . . .

Also try George Andriopoulos's talk:
"The Impact of Innovation Via Disruption"
2018

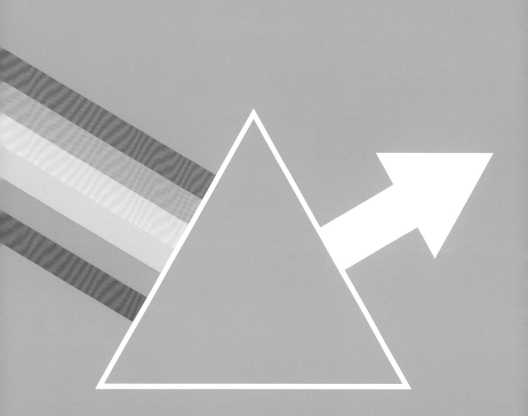

**IT TAKES PEOPLE FROM THE OUTSIDE
TO CHANGE THINGS ON THE INSIDE.
INNOVATION HAPPENS FROM OUTSIDERS.**
RICHIE NORTON, FOUNDER OF GLOBAL CONSULTING CIRCLE

DIVERSITY MEANS INCLUSIVITY

New perspectives can help highlight new needs.

 When proudly showcasing your latest design, have you ever stopped to think that it could be harming the independence of some of your most loyal customers? In her talk, advocate for disability and design Sinéad Burke asks the members of her audience to open their eyes to critical design problems that have been invisible to many for too long.

At 3ft 5in (105 cm) tall, Burke routinely experiences problems with the designed world. Everything from available shoe sizes and clothes to products that inhibit her ability to do things for herself add to her daily frustrations.

By providing the audience with an insight into who she is and the daily struggles that she endures, Burke quickly shows us every design from an entirely new perspective. Many businesses will talk the talk about diversity and inclusion, but few will walk the walk.

Innovation is much more than just another buzzword. It should be about encouraging all of our employees to see the world from an entirely new perspective. Only then can we promote healthy dialogues in an innovative and inclusive environment.

Burke's talk is essential viewing for obtaining a very different perspective on the designed world. After all, that's what innovation is all about.

FIND OUT MORE

Sinéad Burke's talk:
"Why Design Should Include Everyone"
2017
. . . .

"

I OFTEN FORGET THAT I'M A LITTLE PERSON. IT'S THE PHYSICAL ENVIRONMENT AND SOCIETY THAT REMIND ME.

SINÉAD BURKE

INNOVATION IS A MARATHON, NOT A SPRINT

Take steps to become a leader, rather than a follower.

We live in an age of instant gratification where tangible results are delivered on demand. We are surrounded by technological change that is moving forward at a breathtaking speed, and the reality facing every business leader is that it will never move this slowly again. But don't be fooled into believing that the pace of digital development can help you change the world overnight. Instead of focusing on quick fixes for his or her problems, an effective leader must play the long game toward becoming a winning innovator.

81/100
INVEST TIME IN PEOPLE

Develop a culture in which your employees know that you believe in them.

Have you ever asked yourself or your teams, "Why don't we get the best out of people?" In his talks on education, creative expert Sir Ken Robinson argues it's because we've been conditioned to become good workers, rather than innovators. Essentially, we are educating people out of their creativity. Sir Ken also believes that we have a crisis of human resources. The problem is that many people have no real sense of what their talents might be.

Every individual needs to break free from everything he or she knows and find the inner spark that will help them thrive as an innovator. It's your job as a leader to nurture their ability to do this. Have you noticed that when you're doing something you love, an hour feels like five minutes? And if you're doing something that doesn't resonate with your spirit, five minutes feels like an hour? Innovation is hard because it means doing something that people don't find very easy. It means challenging what

we take for granted, things that seem obvious. You also need to accept that it can take time to educate people back into their creativity. For a wider discussion on getting the best from your employees, see Chapter 2.

FIND OUT MORE

Sir Ken Robinson's talks: "Bring on the Learning Revolution!" 2010

"How to Escape Education's Death Valley" 2013

"

HUMAN TALENT IS TREMENDOUSLY DIVERSE. PEOPLE HAVE VERY DIFFERENT APTITUDES. YOU KNOW, TO ME, HUMAN COMMUNITIES DEPEND UPON A DIVERSITY OF TALENT, NOT A SINGULAR CONCEPTION OF ABILITY. "

SIR KEN ROBINSON

PLAY THE LONG GAME

Take your cue from thirty years of tech-fueled innovation.

Technology dominates almost every aspect of our lives, as the dream of a Jetsons' lifestyle slowly becomes a reality. While it may feel as if digital transformations have happened overnight, it actually took a long time to get where we are today.

In his talk, MIT Media Lab founder Nicholas Negroponte takes his audience on a journey through the last thirty years of tech. He also shares his desire to help connect the last billion people located in rural areas in developing countries.

What is Negroponte's bold prediction for the future? The man who predicted CD-ROMs, video teleconferencing, service kiosks, and touchscreens back in 1984 predicts that, in thirty years' time, we will have the ability to ingest information in a pill format. Sure, that might sound crazy, but never dismiss someone with a great track record of saying, I told you so.

The biggest lesson from this talk is that none of these technological revolutions occurred within just a few months, or even years. Changing the world and ensuring that every child has a laptop requires you to play the long game rather than allow yourself to become distracted by quick wins and instant gratification.

Q FIND OUT MORE

Nicholas Negroponte's talk: "A Thirty-Year History of the Future" 2014

> **THERE ARE THREE SORTS OF PEOPLE IN THE WORLD: THOSE WHO ARE IMMOVABLE, PEOPLE WHO DON'T GET IT, OR DON'T WANT TO DO ANYTHING ABOUT IT; THOSE WHO ARE MOVABLE, PEOPLE WHO SEE THE NEED FOR CHANGE AND ARE PREPARED TO LISTEN TO IT; AND THOSE WHO MOVE, PEOPLE WHO MAKE THINGS HAPPEN.**
>
> **BENJAMIN FRANKLIN**

"AHA"

Look for ways to increase the occurrence of those "aha" moments.

> **OUR FUTURE GROWTH RELIES ON COMPETITIVENESS AND INNOVATION, SKILLS AND PRODUCTIVITY, AND THESE, IN TURN, RELY ON THE EDUCATION OF OUR PEOPLE.**
> **JULIA GILLARD, FORMER AUSTRALIAN PRIME MINISTER**

 Cofounder of Blue Man Group, Matt Goldman believes certain conditions create "aha" moments of surprise and learning frequently and intentionally rather than randomly and occasionally (see page 42).

In his talk, Goldman advises that, "We need to cultivate safe and conducive conditions for new and innovative ideas to evolve and thrive." Humans, by their very nature, are born innovators. As Goldman said, if we weren't, we'd all be using the same arrowheads that we were using ten thousand years ago.

As a leader there are several steps you can take to increase the frequency of "aha" moments in your working environment. The first is to make a commitment to investing time in your team. Only then can you build vibrant, collaborative communities that are not afraid to take risks and celebrate mistakes.

Focus on building an environment that embraces multiple perspectives and supports what others need to learn, and find ways to cultivate the practice of self-awareness. When you invest in learning and in building communities in

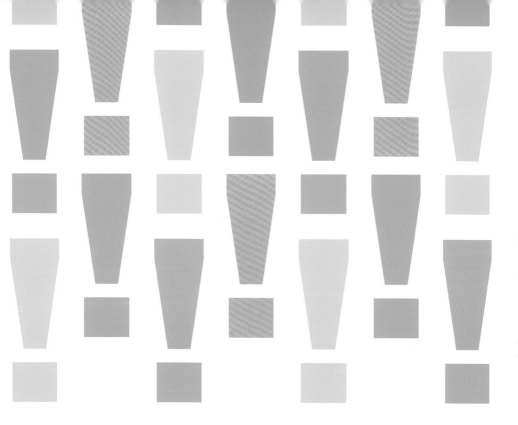

these ways, you will naturally begin reshaping the working environment. You will not only create more "aha" moments, but you will also increase your chances of changing the world.

For further inspiration, consider the youth talk given by Apremya Mithal, who believes that innovation is not only the essence of a changing world but is responsible for changing it, too.

🔍 FIND OUT MORE

Matt Goldman's talk:
"The Search For 'Aha!' Moments"
2017

Also try Apremya Mithal's talk:
"How Innovation Is Changing the World"
2018

THINK LATERALLY

You can always take a less conventional path to enhancing teamwork and creativity.

At the very least, the innovation journey requires you to brush up on your leadership, teamwork, creativity, and negotiation skills, and every successful leader develops a style of his or her own. CEO of software company Boardable, Jeb Banner steps away from corporate speak and reveals how he discovered that everything he knows about business was learned from being in a band.

Musicians are quick learners and problem solvers. They are naturally creative and collaborative. But Banner noticed that in the world of business, organizations struggle with teamwork and creativity. In a world where it can be challenging to get buy-in from cynical employees, Banner took a different approach as he explains in his talk. He asks the audience, what if businesses had employees that were as passionate about their work, as musicians are about their music? His message is that, by inspiring employees with the why of their business, leaders will attract more like-minded employees to that purpose.

Finally, Banner asks that we look at how we teach our children. What if we taught our children not just how to play music, but to write music? It could lead them down all kinds of strange and wonderful paths forming their own bands and having a multitude of important experiences. But maybe it would also help organizations in the future with their struggle with teamwork and creativity.

Q FIND OUT MORE

Jeb Banner's talk:
"Everything I Needed to Know About Business I Learned from Being in a Band"
2013

. . . .

Also try Stanford Thompson's talk:
"Music for Social Innovation"
2012

"ALL CHILDREN ARE BORN ARTISTS, THE PROBLEM IS TO REMAIN AN ARTIST AS WE GROW UP."

PABLO PICASSO

ABOLISH HIERARCHY

Corporate hierachy is an obstacle to innovation.

Hierarchies were created at the dawn of an industrial revolution in a bid to maximize on efficiency and scale. But in our modern, digitally connected world, efficiency pales against the need for innovation, change, and expediency. Increasingly leaders are having to trust the judgment of their employees. More than that, leaders have to provide their employees with the learning tools they need in order to make decisions for themselves.

In her talk, leadership strategist Charlene Li explains that today's business world is less about control and more about empowerment (see page 56). We need to enable employees to acquire the information they need so that they can make their own decisions. A culture of sharing in networks to make critical decisions is the only way that leaders are going to be able to harness the passion, energy, and creativity of their staff.

> **INNOVATION HAS NEVER COME THROUGH BUREAUCRACY AND HIERARCHY. IT'S ALWAYS COME FROM INDIVIDUALS.**
> **MALCOLM FORBES, ENTREPRENEUR**

🔍 FIND OUT MORE

Charlene Li's talk:
"Efficient Leadership in the Digital Era
2014

....

Also try Markus Reitzig's talk:
"How Hierarchies Help and Hamper Us in Creating Great Organizations"
2016

SPACE TO CREATE

Innovation requires a dedicated area for teams to share projects and ideas.

Marketing and healthcare expert Robin Hooker grew up tinkering in his father's workshop and always had the luxury of access to a small space that enabled him to reimagine the world. This ability to modify, repair, and experiment to his heart's content is something that would stay with him for life.

However, it wasn't until he reached adulthood that he realized there weren't many people who grew up with access to what he likes to call "makerspaces."

Many will argue that you cannot teach people to innovate. However, having somewhere that encourages the collision of ideas and a designated area for collaboration can accelerate your innovation efforts and provide magical results. In his talk, Hooker explains why he believes that makerspaces allow people in digital communities to bring more of their ideas to life. While equipment is important, these spaces are really about people. Hooker quips, "There's a saying in the maker movement. They came for the tools, but they stayed for the people."

> **ALL WORK AND NO PLAY DOESN'T JUST MAKE JILL AND JACK DULL, IT KILLS THE POTENTIAL OF DISCOVERY, MASTERY, AND OPENNESS TO CHANGE AND FLEXIBILITY AND IT HINDERS INNOVATION AND INVENTION.**
> **JOLINE GODFREY, FOUNDER OF THE UNEXPECTED TABLE**

🔍 FIND OUT MORE

Robin Hooker's talk:
"A Makerspace for Everyone"
2018

....

Also try Nati Sang's talk:
"Maker's Spaces: Spaces for Learning and Innovation"
2018

LOOK AROUND YOU

You are surrounded by innovation.

Innovation is a mind-set, a process, and a journey. We have looked at the importance of setting aside some space where a community can embrace innovation (see page 163). Sir Ken Robinson also warned how education removed our ability to create and be more innovative (see page 154).

In her talk, entrepreneur Mei Tan talks about the journey of innovation in her life. She also reminds her audience that everything in our universe was created and innovated by human beings. Business leaders can immerse themselves in this world by adopting a new mind-set and leveraging technology.

If you are learning to innovate yourself, you may find many of the answers you seek were discovered during your childhood. Tan advises that we all need to remember to be curious and learn to be different. And most importantly, to be innovative. For inspiration, take a look around you and see that innovation can be applied anywhere.

For those wondering how to inspire and unleash the innovators of tomorrow, check out Stephen Brand's talk for some simple, yet effective advice.

FIND OUT MORE

Mei Tan's talk:
"Journey of Innovation in Life"
2019
. . . .
Also try Stephen Brand's talk:
"The Innovator's Journey"
2017

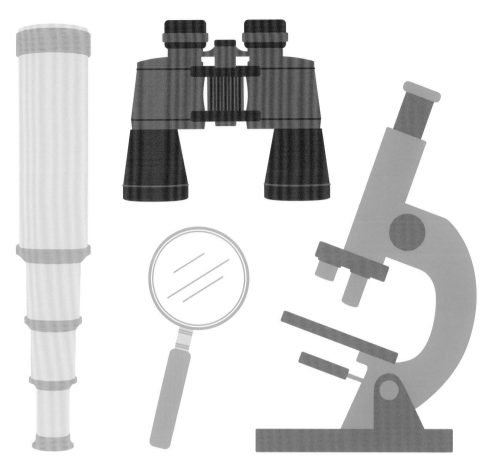

DREAMERS ARE MOCKED AS IMPRACTICAL. THE TRUTH IS THEY ARE THE MOST PRACTICAL, AS THEIR INNOVATIONS LEAD TO PROGRESS AND A BETTER WAY OF LIFE FOR ALL OF US.
ROBIN SHARMA, LEADERSHIP EXPERT

YOU, TOO, CAN INNOVATE

What is holding you back?

Jay Martin is a serial entrepreneur who is on a mission to change the world through innovation and to teach others how to do the same. In his talk, Martin tells his audience that everyone can use innovation to directly impact their lives and the lives of those around them.

Martin also speaks of how he believes we not only have an opportunity but a responsibility to use innovation to bring positive change to the world. Whether we develop new technologies, ways of using technology, or exploring how we can improve our business, we must learn and grow as we move forward. But patiently.

Entire teams must learn to view the world through a mind that is free to imagine, without limitations. Only then can they genuinely understand the issues and the opportunities at hand. This will help them identify a problem and turn an idea into a solution. Everyone can innovate and invent. The creativity of innovation stems from our passion for making a difference.

It's time to invest in yourself and your teams to ensure that your innovation efforts will last a lot longer than just a few months.

> **I BELIEVE INNOVATION IS THE MOST POWERFUL FORCE FOR CHANGE IN THE WORLD.**
> **BILL GATES**

Q FIND OUT MORE

Jay Martin's talk:
"Teaching the World to Innovate"
2011

THE POWER OF COMMUNITY

Don't forget to look beyond your own objectives.

Better known as the godfather of street skating, Rodney Mullen is one of the most influential skateboarders in history. But his talk "Pop an Ollie and Innovate" is about more than skateboarding. He talks about adapting to different cultures and using existing skills to innovate and create something new.

Mullen sets the scene by telling his audience that once you know the technology inside out, you can manipulate it and steer it to do things it was never intended to do. The ethos of an innovative community is to take what others do, make it better, and give it back so everyone can rise together.

There's an intrinsic value in creating something for the sake of creating it. But he went on to add that there is something special about dropping it into a community of your own making. Seeing it dispersed, and seeing younger, more talented individuals take it to levels you could never imagine, helps it lives on.

Innovation leadership is not all about technology or your personal goals. Sometimes it's about being something much bigger than your innovation strategy and being part of a community that can see the bigger picture.

> **NEVER DOUBT THAT A SMALL GROUP OF THOUGHTFUL, COMMITTED CITIZENS CAN CHANGE THE WORLD. INDEED, IT IS THE ONLY THING THAT EVER HAS.**
>
> MARGARET MEAD, CULTURAL ANTHROPOLOGIST

Q FIND OUT MORE

Rodney Mullen's talks:
"Pop an Ollie and Innovate!"
2012

"On Getting Up Again"
2013

PLAY FAIR

Promoting a culture of fairness is critical to your innovation plans.

> **MY MODEL FOR BUSINESS IS THE BEATLES. THEY WERE FOUR GUYS WHO KEPT EACH OTHER'S KIND OF NEGATIVE TENDENCIES IN CHECK. THEY BALANCED EACH OTHER, AND THE TOTAL WAS GREATER THAN THE SUM OF ITS PARTS. THAT'S HOW I SEE BUSINESS. GREAT THINGS IN BUSINESS ARE NEVER DONE BY ONE PERSON. THEY'RE DONE BY A TEAM OF PEOPLE.**
>
> **STEVE JOBS**

Innovation is misunderstood and feared by many organizations, who foolishly think that it's a rare gift only enjoyed by the privileged few in leadership roles. But the secret to success involves identifying the talents within your entire team. Only then can you work through the innovation process together.

Individuals seldom drive innovation; it takes a collaborative environment to change organizational behavior (see page 32). In his talk, Marco Alverà explains how his company works to create a culture of fairness that taps into our innate sense of what's right and wrong.

If you are serious about getting the best out of people, show them how much you care. That is the moment where they will leave their fears behind and bring their authentic selves to work. The reason why every leader isn't making fairness a priority is baffling.

Kevin Cahill hammers home a similar message in his talk. He asks his audience to imagine the possibilities of a world

powered by teamwork, guided by
a culture of "we" not "me" thinking.

   Innovation is much bigger than your
organization, leadership, and corporate
vision. Motivation, creativity, and teamwork
are the areas where you need to focus the
most. Get the balance right, and you too
can set yourself apart as an effective
leader in innovation.

Q FIND OUT MORE

Marco Alverà's talk:
"The Surprising Ingredient that
Makes Businesses Work Better"
2018

Also try Kevin Cahill's talk:
"Teamwork Reimagined"
 2017

INFLUENTIAL INNOVATORS

Use this opportunity to learn from the world's greatest innovators.

You now have all the tools you need on your innovation journey. You should be able to open your eyes and see the world differently and from multiple perspectives. It's down to you to use a combination of these skills and your passion for creating something new to solve real problems. Although it might feel daunting at first, you have nothing to fear. You can follow in the footsteps of some of the greatest innovators of our time, people who have left a clear path. Learn from their mistakes, and don't be afraid to make your own. Your missteps may lead to your greatest innovations.

THINK BIGGER

Elon Musk urges the global community to think beyond planet Earth.

Elon Musk is possibly one of the most exciting innovators alive today. He seems to have everything covered from innovative transport to space exploration. Musk even famously launched a Tesla Roadster into space using planet Earth as the ultimate backdrop, which was arguably a work of art, too.

Musk has spoken in two talks. The first was in 2013 where the founder of PayPal, Tesla Motors, and SpaceX shared his vision for the future with TED curator Chris Anderson. The conversation covered everything from mass-marketed electric cars to reusable rockets and solar energy.

The man that many compare to a real-life Tony Stark returned to the talks stage in 2017. Once again, he chatted with Chris Anderson about digging tunnels under LA, SpaceX, and his motivation for building a future on Mars.

Despite his increasing list of mind-blowing innovations, Musk's most exciting gift to the world is that of enabling global citizens of all ages to think bigger. By looking at our world differently and even from space, maybe we can all remove the self-imposed limitations that have been restricting our ambitions.

Q FIND OUT MORE

Elon Musk's talks:
"The Mind Behind Tesla, SpaceX, SolarCity"
2013

. . . .

"The Future We're Building
—and Boring"
2017

"

BEING ABLE TO TALK TO PEOPLE OVER LONG DISTANCES, TO TRANSMIT IMAGES, FLYING, ACCESSING VAST AMOUNTS OF DATA LIKE AN ORACLE. THESE ARE ALL THINGS THAT WOULD HAVE BEEN CONSIDERED MAGIC A FEW HUNDRED YEARS AGO. "

ELON MUSK

CHANGING THE WORLD

People with an innovative mind-set can change the world.

Bill Gates famously changed the world with Microsoft. His success was driven by his dream to enable millions of people to realize their potential through great software. Gates continues his journey to improve the world today, armed with his passion for innovation and philanthropy.

Gates has graced the talks stage six times. He delivered one of his most memorable talks, "Innovating to Zero," in 2010, where he unveiled his vision for the world's energy future, which centered on an ambitious mission to make zero carbon emissions globally by 2050.

Anyone who dismissed Gates's warning of planetary catastrophe a decade ago can no longer deny the dangers that lie ahead. Energy and climate are more important to the global community than anything else on our tiny planet.

On my daily tech podcast, I always say that technology works best when it brings people together. This is partly inspired by Gates and how he is using tech to help the poorest two billion on our planet live better lives. As an innovator, it's your responsibility to be the change that you want to see in the world.

> ## INNOVATION IS THE PROCESS OF CREATING SOMETHING NEW THAT MAKES LIFE BETTER. INNOVATION IS IMPOSSIBLE WITHOUT PASSION. INNOVATORS SEE THE WORLD DIFFERENTLY.
>
> **BILL GATES**

Q FIND OUT MORE

Bill Gates's talk:
"Innovating to Zero"
2010

CHALLENGE YOURSELF

It is possible to find a voice outside of your comfort zone.

Long before taking the role of COO at Facebook in 2008, Sheryl Sandberg built and managed Google's successful online sales and operations program. Having earned her success in a famously male-dominated industry, Sandberg is a highly respected tech innovator.

In her 2010 talk, she asks the question, why is there a smaller percentage of women than men reaching the top of their professions? Sandberg goes on to share her insights and advice to enable women to secure a role in the C-suite.

Four years later she returned to the talks stage with millions of views and a best-selling book under her belt and spoke of why many women still struggle with success. Sandberg also touches on her battles with her own success.

She explains how she had never expected to write a book. "I'm not an author, I'm not a writer." But she quickly learned how her book and videos of her talk were impacting people's lives. In bravely stepping outside of her comfort zone, Sandberg not only found her voice, but helped us do the same.

Although it's easy to get sidetracked with your own mission, remember that it's not all about you. Genuine innovators value innovation and help others on their journey too.

> **WE MUST RAISE BOTH THE CEILING AND THE FLOOR.**
> **SHERYL SANDBERG**

Q FIND OUT MORE

Sheryl Sandberg's talks:
"Why We Have Too Few Women Leaders"
2010

"So, We Leaned in . . . Now What?"
2014

A SENSE OF PURPOSE

Intelligence is the ability to adapt to change.

Where did we come from? Are we alone in the universe? What is the future of the human race? These are just a few of the questions that many of us think about. Professor Stephen Hawking also tackles such questions in his 2008 talk.

Hawking offers a warning that our only chance of long-term survival is not to remain looking inwardly on planet Earth, but to spread out into space. He goes on to say that he feels lucky that his disability has not been a serious handicap. "Indeed, it has probably given me more time than most people to pursue the quest for knowledge."

Stephen Hawking was science's brightest star and will be remembered for being one of the greatest minds of our time. In questioning the universe, he quickly realized that time is our most precious resource and that making mistakes is important. On this same subject, Hawking once famously quipped, "without imperfection, neither you nor I would exist."

Hawking was an eternal optimist and had a great sense of humor. He taught me to have a sense of purpose, never to give up, and always to be curious—all of which are the essential traits required to innovate.

Q FIND OUT MORE

Stephen Hawking's talk:
"Questioning the Universe"
2008
. . . .

> **REMEMBER TO LOOK UP AT THE STARS AND NOT DOWN AT YOUR FEET. TRY TO MAKE SENSE OF WHAT YOU SEE AND WONDER ABOUT WHAT MAKES THE UNIVERSE EXIST. BE CURIOUS. AND HOWEVER DIFFICULT LIFE MAY SEEM, THERE IS ALWAYS SOMETHING YOU CAN DO AND SUCCEED AT. IT MATTERS THAT YOU DON'T JUST GIVE UP.**
>
> **STEPHEN HAWKING**

FIND NEW WAYS TO SOLVE OLD PROBLEMS

Steve Wozniak shares innovation lessons from Apple's early days.

> **TRY TO THINK OF NEW WAYS TO SOLVE OLD PROBLEMS. VERY OFTEN WE LOOK AT SOMETHING WE HAVE AND SAY; I COULD MAKE IT BETTER. THAT'S INNOVATION.**
> **STEVE WOZNIAK**

Steve Wozniak was one of the three founders of Apple Computer Company, setting up in Steve Jobs' garage back in 1976. Affectionately known as Woz, the Silicon Valley icon and philanthropist helped shape the computing industry with his design of Apple's first line of products. But what did he learn about innovation?

In his talk, Woz tells his audience how traditional education teaches us rules. But, our desire for openness and greater learning is inhibited. You can only learn what is in this class, the same thing on the same days as every other student in your class. School teaches us that intelligence is having the same correct answer that everyone else in the class has.

If you dare to question anything, you are labeled disruptive. Woz goes on to highlight that learning to think for yourself and coming up with your own ideas is the heart of innovation. There are two talks that provide unique insights into the days at Apple with Steve Jobs, the technology, and social revolution that they created together.

Anyone looking to learn from these legendary innovators only needs to consider another revealing quote from Woz. "Our first computers were born not out of greed or ego, but in the revolutionary spirit of helping common people rise above the most powerful institutions." For me personally, this sums up what innovation is all about.

Q FIND OUT MORE

Steve Wozniak's talks:
"Technology and Social Revolution"
2012
. . . .
"The Early Days"
2015

TAKE CONTROL OF YOUR DESTINY

Gary Vaynerchuk offers a few motivational words.

Gary Vaynerchuk is an innovative and influential straight-talking entrepreneur. He cares most passionately about his community and constantly reminds his followers to stop caring what other people think. For Vaynerchuk, innovation isn't a tactic. It's a religion.

In 2006 Vaynerchuk launched Wine Library TV, a daily video blog about wine. As his audience grew and word spread of his informal and unorthodox attitude to wine, his innovative approach and infectious enthusiasm quickly captured the attention of the global community.

At the Web 2.0 Expo in 2008, Vaynerchuk gave an inspiring talk advising his audience to overcome self-doubt and secure their own successes. Vaynerchuk advised everyone to stop doing things they hate and refocus their efforts on patience and passion.

What about the future? When I met Vaynerchuk, I asked him how emerging technologies such as Blockchain will affect businesses. He replied, "Anybody in the middle, from the person that makes the product to the person that consumes the product, is vulnerable. Technology is coming after you, and if you're in the middle, you need to pay attention to that statement."

Before you set out on your innovation journey, Vaynerchuk offers one final piece of advice. "Your legacy is being written by yourself. So, make the right decisions."

Q FIND OUT MORE

Gary Vaynerchuk's talk:
"Do What You Love (No Excuses!)"
2008
· ·

" YOU NEED TO SPEND ALL OF YOUR TIME AND ENERGY ON CREATING SOMETHING THAT ACTUALLY BRINGS VALUE TO THE PEOPLE YOU'RE ASKING FOR MONEY! "

GARY VAYNERCHUK

GIVE INNOVATION A CHANCE

The element of chance will help you innovate.

Tim Berners-Lee invented the World Wide Web and it's fair to say that he knows a thing or two about innovation. His invention was a solution to the problems associated with orchestrating and tracking complex, collaborative projects in the 1980s.

It has been thirty years since Berners-Lee set out to reframe the way we use the information and the ways in which we work together. It all began with a written memo suggesting the development of a global hypertext system, although nobody did anything with it.

Eighteen months later, his boss said he could do it on the side, as a sort of a play project, and the rest is history. In his talk, "The Next Web," Berners-Lee explains that this is how innovation happens. Serendipity played a part in many inventions, from penicillin to the Segway super scooter and the World Wide Web. Structured innovation processes can help generate creative ideas. But do not underestimate how the element of chance will play a much bigger role than you realize.

"INNOVATION IS SERENDIPITY, SO YOU DON'T KNOW WHAT PEOPLE WILL MAKE."
TIM BERNERS-LEE

Q FIND OUT MORE

Tim Berners-Lee's talks:
"The Next Web"
2009

....

"The Year Open Data Went Worldwide"
2010

....

"A Magna Carta for the Web"
2014

LESSONS FROM JEFF BEZOS

Are you willing to be misunderstood?

Jeff Bezos might not have invented online shopping, but since the Amazon.com bookstore was launched in 1994, it has changed the way people shop all over the world. One-click shopping, user reviews, and quick delivery to our homes are also responsible for raising our expectations to an entirely new level.

These innovations have set a new standard with which every business must compete. Many have compared the early days of the internet with the California Gold Rush. Back in 2007, companies believed that they had missed their window of opportunity and that the nugget of gold had been taken. In his talk, Bezos advises "the good thing with innovation is there isn't a last nugget. Every new thing creates two new questions and two new opportunities." Simply follow your curiosity and passions and you will find a way to improve things.

More recently Bezos talked about how Amazon faced a huge backlash from stakeholders when they first allowed customers to post reviews of books. He advises, "If you're going to do anything new or innovative, you have to be willing to be misunderstood."

> **THERE ARE TWO WAYS TO EXTEND A BUSINESS. TAKE INVENTORY OF WHAT YOU'RE GOOD AT AND EXTEND OUT FROM YOUR SKILLS. OR DETERMINE WHAT YOUR CUSTOMERS NEED AND WORK BACKWARD, EVEN IF IT REQUIRES LEARNING NEW SKILLS. KINDLE IS AN EXAMPLE OF WORKING BACKWARD.**
> **JEFF BEZOS**

🔍 FIND OUT MORE

Jeff Bezos's talk:
"The Electricity Metaphor for the Web's Future"
2007

THE INNOVATIVE SPIRIT

You can change our world for the better.

Innovation is all about expanding your horizons and thinking beyond your own goals. Through her innovative work, Dr. Jane Goodall altered scientific thinking about the relationship between humans and other mammals. She was even dubbed by her biographer as "the woman who redefined man."

As one of the world's greatest innovators, Goodall was able to change our perceptions of primates, people, and the connection between the two. In her 2003 talk, she explores what separates humans from chimpanzees. She advises that we're the ones who can make a difference. In her follow up talk in 2007, she advises by thinking differently, animals and humans can live together.

Our indomitable human spirit plays a big part in how we successfully innovate. Goodall spoke of the inspiring determination of people that have been battered by poverty, disease, or whatever, but they manage to pull themselves up out of it. Despite whatever life throws at people, they still take their part in changing the world.

Goodall's work has enabled community projects and innovation labs that help people in African towns live side-by-side with threatened animals. To keep your innovative spirit alive you will need to be imaginative, persistent, flexible, and armed with dogged determination to succeed

> ❝
> **WHAT YOU DO MAKES A DIFFERENCE, AND YOU HAVE TO DECIDE WHAT KIND OF DIFFERENCE YOU WANT TO MAKE.** ❞
> **JANE GOODALL**

🔍 FIND OUT MORE

Jane Goodall's talks:
"What Separates Us From Chimpanzees?"
2003

. . . .

"How Humans and Animals Can Live Together"
2007

THIRTY THOUSAND FEET AND BEYOND

Sir Richard Branson shares his vision for making a difference.

Sir Richard Branson has floated down the Thames River with the Sex Pistols, ballooned across the Atlantic Ocean, and can now be found taking the lead in the space race. He is less interested in leaving a legacy behind and much more motivated by being able to make a difference. His upbringing taught him that if he is in a position to radically change other people's lives for the better, it's his responsibility to do it.

In his talk, Branson explains how he looks at life as one long learning process. "If I fly on somebody else's airline and find the experience is not a pleasant one, which it wasn't . . . then I'd think, well, you know, maybe I can create the kind of airline that I'd like to fly on. And so, I got a second-hand 747 from Boeing and gave it a go."

Branson has been wowing his customers with innovative experiences before the experience economy was even a thing. How did he do it? He built a team that loves what they do and set out to do things differently from his competitors.

You now have all the information that you need to innovate for yourself. Maybe you can give it a go just like Branson. But remember to share your journey with others, too.

> **INNOVATION HAPPENS WHEN PEOPLE ARE GIVEN THE FREEDOM TO ASK QUESTIONS AND THE RESOURCES AND POWER TO FIND THE ANSWERS.**
> **RICHARD BRANSON**

Q FIND OUT MORE

Richard Branson's talk:
"Life at Thirty Thousand Feet"
2007

. . . .

INDEX OF SPEAKERS AND THEIR TALKS

Unless another website has been stated, the TED talks below can be accessed via the TED website by typing www.ted.com/talks followed by the speaker specific link, for example www.ted.com/talks /susan_cain_the_power_of_introverts.

INDEX

ACKNOWLEDGMENTS

During my IT career, I felt compelled to help the department develop as a team of innovative business enablers rather than a team of blockers who always said no. They say you become the average of the people you spend the most time with, so I surrounded myself with members of the global online community who felt the same way that I do about innovation. Writers such as John White, Paul Drury, Dustin McKissen, and Sarah Elkins enabled me to see how the secret to innovation is having people and technology working seamlessly side by side.

After winning a LinkedIn Top Voice Award for my writing in 2015, I was fortunate enough to speak with an eclectic list of people such as William Shatner, Wendy Williams, Guy Kawasaki, John Sculley, and Marylene Delbourg-Delphis about their personal experiences with innovation. Their stories played a huge part in my inspiration for this book. Innovation is a journey not a destination. Embedding a culture of innovation takes a great deal of time and commitment. I would like to thank Dr. Amantha Imber for teaching me this, along with how to develop and sustain a culture of innovation.

I must thank my wife Kerry for her unwavering support in all that I do. Not to mention putting up with me watching hundreds of hours of TED Talks and kicking me out of bed at 5:30 a.m. to ensure that I met my deadlines. The birth of my son inspired me to be a better man, and Samantha taught me to make the most of every day that we have on this tiny planet.

Kirstie Marsden deserves a special mention for inspiring me with her work ethic, along with "Olympic Five" for helping me keep my feet on the ground, while reaching for the stars. Finally a special thank you to Anna Southgate who helped me bring my ideas to life in this book and keep me on the right track every step of the way.

What I am trying to say is that innovation is about people, rather than technology. I believe that businesses should focus more on the potential hidden inside their teams of potential innovators and less on innovation itself. Combine that with technology, and you are on the right track.

PICTURE CREDITS

p150 – Vecteezy.com / Freepik.com
p173 – iStock.com/jack0m